Tō eallum mīnum lārēowum

An Index

of Theme and Image

To the Homilies

of the Anglo-Saxon Church

*Comprising the Homilies of
Ælfric, Wulfstan, and the
Blickling and Vercelli Codices*

Tᶱ

Published 1995

Published by
Anglo-Saxon Books
Frithgarth
Thetford Forest Park
Hockwold cum Wilton
Norfolk England

Printed by
Antony Rowe Ltd.
Chippenham
Wiltshire
England

British Library Catologuing-in-Publication Data. A catalogue record for this
book is available from the British Library.

ISBN 1-898281-05-X

CONTENTS

INTRODUCTION

This index is intended to serve as a guide to the fundamental themes and images that inform the Old English homilies. Anyone studying these texts must contend with their often loosely associative manner, which can lend them an encyclopaedic (though not always systematic) breadth of topic and allusion. The Anglo-Saxon homilist can proceed from point to point in a fashion internally consistent yet sometimes rather surprising to the modern mind. As a result, one can never anticipate all that a homily may contain simply on the basis of its title (if it has one) or its occasion (ditto). The seventeenth piece in Ælfric's *Lives of the Saints* (to take an almost random example) gathers into its ample embrace references to the Law and the Spirit, the torments of hell, lists of sins and sinners, idolatry, sortilege and augury, the uses of the Lord's Prayer and the Creed as travel charms, Simon Magus, animism, infanticide, medicine, love potions, exorcism, fate and free will, foreknowledge, and animal psychology – among other concerns. The attentive mind, once confronted with it, will no doubt discern the pattern governing this disparate array, but who could have guessed it in advance?

It has thus been necessary for the researcher to pursue one or both of two courses when investigating the Old English homilies: either read them all (usually more than once) or, at least recently, conduct key-word searches through the microfiche concordance published by the Old English Dictionary project at the University of Toronto. Both paths are beset by peculiar perils: lost time and cross-eyed exhaustion along the first, and along the second the constant worry that your key-words will simply not have taken you everywhere you needed to go, not to mention the high chaff-to-wheat ratio of key-word searches. Neither set of difficulties is utterly insurmountable, but I hope this index should make both of them less inevitable.

A major challenge in compiling this index has been how to define 'theme' and 'image'; in the end, after several false starts, I found the only sane way to proceed: rather than impose some eventually Procrustean *a priori* definition, I let the homilists themselves lead me, so that each entry in the pages that follow represents a thing, a concept, a doctrine, a narrative, or a symbol or anything else that held enough significance for a homilist to engage his attention for more than a passing mention. It being patently inconvenient to title the result *An Index of Things, Concepts, Doctrines, Narratives, Symbols, and Anything Else in Old English Homilies*, 'theme and image' has persisted in my mind as a convenient shorthand.

The index is in no way comprehensive or exhaustive. I have aimed instead at making it as *useful* as possible – for example, under the entry 'The Fall of Adam and Eve' will be found not every single mention of or allusion to that event, many of which would be bare mentions without any development or discussion, but only those containing what I have judged to be a potentially significant degree of narration, exposition, or interpretation, something that contributes to the literary effect of a passage or that reveals something of its author's patterns of thought and design. An ineradicably subjective element inheres in all such judgements, as it does in how I have identified the boundaries of individual citations: it is not always possible to say in a given text where a particular theme or image begins and ends, and at least some of my choices may seem arbitrary.

For many decades now, the Old English homilies have been industriously mined for their theological and linguistic contents, but they have yet to receive their full measure of attention as literary artefacts (however odd the notion might have seemed to their authors), in part, I suspect, because of the extraordinary labours involved in getting acquainted with them fully. Thus it is chiefly, though by no means exclusively, the student and the scholar of medieval literature that I have had in mind in compiling this index, for whom I hope it will help to open up the homilies more fully to their study and imagination. If I have accomplished anything else, I hope it might be that amplitude and those possibilities for serendipity that distinguish many of the indices of scholarly works from previous centuries.

ABBREVIATIONS

B *The Blickling Homilies.* Ed. R. Morris. 1874-1880 (Early English Text Society 58, 63, 73). Rpt. in 1 vol. Oxford: Oxford U P, 1967.[1]

CHI *The Homilies of the Anglo-Saxon Church. The First Part, Containing the Sermones Catholici or Homilies of Ælfric. In the Original Anglo-Saxon, with an English Version.* Vol. I. Ed. Benjamin Thorpe. London: the Aelfric Society, 1844.[1]

CHII *Ælfric's Catholic Homilies: The Second Series.* Ed. Malcolm Godden. London and New York: Oxford U P (Early English Text Society ss 5), 1979.

LS *Ælfric's Lives of Saints: Being a Set of Sermons on Saints' Days formerly observed by the English Church.* Ed. Walter W. Skeat. 1881–1900 (Early English Text Society 76, 82, 94, 114). Rpt. in 2 vols. (nos. 76 and 82 as vol. 1, nos. 94 and 114 as vol. 2) Oxford: Oxford U P, 1966.

Supp *Homilies of Ælfric: A Supplementary Collection.* 2 vols. Ed. John Pope. London and New York: Oxford U P (Early English Text Society 259, 260), 1967, 1968.

V *The Vercelli Homilies.* Ed. Donald G. Scragg. Oxford: Oxford U P (Early English Text Society 300), 1992.

Vf *Die Vercelli Homilien* [homilies 1–8]. Ed. Max Förster. 1932. Rpt. Darmstadt: Wissenschaftlice Buchgesellschaft, 1964.[2]

---

[1] Citations from these texts are identified by homily and page number. Citations from all other texts are identified by homily and line number.

[2] Since Scragg's edition has been only recently published and the editions of Förster and Szarmach are likely to remain in use for some time at least, for each citation from the Vercelli homilies I first give its location in Scragg's edition, then its location in either Förster or Szarmach in parentheses.

Vs   *Vercelli Homilies ix-xxiii*. Ed. Paul E. Szarmach. Toronto: U of Toronto P, 1981.[2]

W   *The Homilies of Wulfstan*. Ed. Dorothy Bethurum. Oxford: Clarendon P, 1957.

Cross references, if any, are given immediately after each entry. Citations follow each sub-entry in alphabetical order of abbreviation; sub-entries follow the order of their first citations.[3] Citations in **boldface** indicate that the entire homily is concerned in some form with the image or theme in question.

---

[3] Except in entries where I have listed narrations and/or general expositions; these will be listed before all other sub-entries regardless of alphabetical order.

AN INDEX OF
THEME AND IMAGE

An Index of
Theme and Image

A

ABSOLUTION: *see* FORGIVENESS, REPENTANCE.

ABSTINENCE: *see also* ASCETICISM, CHASTITY, CONTINENCE, FASTING; a remedy for gluttony, V 20.80-81 (Vs 20.64); brings men close to God, V 22.163-65 (Vs 22.129-30).

ACTIVE LIFE: *see also* CONTEMPLATIVE LIFE, LABOUR, MONKS, TEACHING; signified by Martha, CHII 29.36-109; will have an end, CHII 29.54-70; signified by two at a grindstone, Supp 18.110-40.

ADULTERY: *see also* DIVORCE, FORNICATION, MARRIAGE, SEXUALITY, SIN, WOMAN; of Herod, CHI 32.484; associated with strife and envy, CHI 39.604; in the decalogue, CHII 12.317-20; under old and new law, Supp 15.90-98.

ADVENT: *see* THE INCARNATION, THE NATIVITY.

AGRICULTURE: *see also* ANIMALS, HERBS; God as a farmer, CHI 24.342; land and its produce only lent by God, CHII 7.80-85, V 10.164-76 (Vs 10.124-33); cultivation signifies humility and repentance, CHII 26.101-10; ploughing signifies good works, Supp 16.116-20; signifies teaching, Supp 18.141-99; Church is God's field, Supp 18.146-52; ploughmen signify bishops and priests, Supp 18.153-68; ripening of fruits and grains signifies human maturation, Supp 19.22-25; a consequence of the fall, Supp 21.51; Old Testament injunctions on first fruits, Supp 30.75-114; earth withholds its crops to punish sin, W 3.40-41.

ALMSGIVING: *see also* GOOD WORKS, POVERTY, TITHING, WEALTH; general expositions, B 4.41-43, 49-53, CHI 11.180, **CHI 23**, CHI 27.398, CHII 7.38-128, Supp 16.146-203, Supp 30.29-68, V 3.143-58 (Vf 3.156-72), V 10.122-99 (Vs 10.92-149), W 10c.159-64, W 13.70-79; and

13

from prison, CHI 34.516-18, CHI 37.574, CHII 24.6-25; set the boundaries of nations, CHI 34.518; their different roles, CHI 36.538-40; appear in disguise to St Cuthbert, CHII 10.28-47; attend the souls of the dying, CHII 20.39-155, Supp 11.181-84, Supp 27.48-70; conduct Dryhthelm through the afterlife, **CHII 21**; rescue unbaptized heathen from death, CHII 34.94-105; St Sebastian teaches from an angel's book, LS 5.89-104; refuse embrace of unbaptized person, LS 5.299-302; protect St Agnes' chastity, LS 7.148-53; signify Christ, Supp 2.115-24; Christ angels' food, Supp 20.128-31; angel carries Habakkuk to Daniel, Supp 21.464-84; heathen gods originally angels, Supp 21.658-63; devils retain some of their former angelic powers, Supp 29.97-104; devils can impersonate, Supp 29.105-10; men now resemble, V 5.190-91 (Vf 5.214-15).

ANIMALS: *see also* AGRICULTURE, ASS, BEES, BIRDS, CAMEL, CREATION, DOG, DRAGON, ELEPHANT, FISH, FOX, HART, HORSE, LAMB, LION, OX, SCORPION, SEAL, SERPENT, SHEEP, SWINE, WOLF; Christ would have assumed their form had it been necessary, B 3.29; Adam names, CHI 1.14, V 19.23-29 (Vs 19.19-23); lack souls, CHI 1.16, CHI 6.96, CHI 20.276, CHI 21.302, CHII 19.178-81, LS 1.25-28, 96-100, 148-49, LS 17.241-52, V 4.77-82 (Vf 4.87-92); animal skins signify death, CHI 1.18; dangerous animals created to punish sin, CHI 6.102, LS 1.222-24; do not harm saints and contemplatives, CHI 6.102, CHI 32.486-88, CHII 33.175-88, LS 4.399-407, LS 23B.761-95, LS 24.40-57, LS 30.413-20, LS 35.253-306, LS 37.231-49; unclean animals signify human impurity, CHI 9.138, LS 10.96-106; gospel preaching signified by untying an animal, CHI 14.208; Jewish animal sacrifice, CHI 28.406, CHII 12.160-64, 344-73, CHII 30.188-90, CHII 32.60-67, LS 10.222-31; animal sacrifice no longer allowed, CHI 38.590, CHII 30.188-90; animal skins signify saints, CHII 15.306-309; St Martin exorcizes, CHII 34.259-61, LS 31.1038-55; nature of, LS 1.49-61; in Jewish dietary law, LS 10.77-95, LS 25.35-107; unclean animals signify the heathen, LS 10.96-106; symbols of the four evangelists, LS 15.178-214; ruminants signify those who ponder and obey God's will, LS 25.47-49; non-ruminants signify those who resist God, LS 25.50-54; clean animals signify the faithful, LS 25.55-60; created as food for men, Supp 1.209-18; men who abuse reason resemble,

Supp 16.57-71; animals at the Nativity signify Christians, V 5.139-50 (Vf 5.156-68).

THE ANNUNCIATION: *see also* THE NATIVITY [appendix 1: MARY (MOTHER OF JESUS), GABRIEL]; narrated, **B 1**, CHI 1.24, **CHI 13**, Supp 11a.61-68, W 7.38-49.

ANTICHRIST: *see also* APOSTASY, THE DAY OF JUDGEMENT, THE DEVIL, HERESY, THE LAST DAYS, PERSECUTION; general expositions, **W 1b, W 4, W 5**; is yet to come, B 11.117; son of the devil, CHI pref.4, W 4.6-11, W 5.66-69; God will permit his evil, CHI pref.4-6, W 4.17-24; his false miracles, CHI pref.4-6, CHII 30.93-97, W 4.43-66; Enoch and Elijah will oppose, CHI 21.308, LS 16.16-21; persecutions during reign of, LS 35.346-60; length of his rule, Supp 18.366-75; time of his advent, **Supp 28**, W 20C.7-9, W 20EI.7-11; identified with the devil, V 2.34-36 (Vf 2.40-43), W 4.43-52; is God's enemy, W 1b.1-12; the sinful are his limbs, W 1b.12-15; his time is now, W 5.36-37; his birth contrasted with Christ's, W 5.37-40; will claim to be Christ, W 5.75-81; deceitfulness of, W 9.113-49.

APOSTASY: *see also* DECEIT, ERROR, FAITH, HERESY, IDOLATRY, TEACHING; during the last days,

CHI pref.4, Supp 18.322-25, V 15.31-38 (Vs 15.26-31), W 4.15-17; signified by a scorpion, CHI 18.252; of the emperor Julian, CHI 30.448, LS 3.289-91; backsliders signified by swine, CHII 23.177-94; of early Christians, LS 5.21-60, Supp 14.140-46; English apostates turning to Norse paganism, Supp 14.126-39; signified by falling stars, W 3.50-53.

THE APOSTLES: *see also* SCRIPTURE, TEACHING [appendix 1: individual apostles by name]; expected restoration of Israel, B 11.117; their mission and labours, B 11.119-21, CHI 21.310, CHI 31.460, CHI 36.542, CHI 38.576, CHII 25.97-110, CHII 35.1-13, CHII 38.179-91, V 7.27-31 (Vf 7.29-33); orphaned at the Ascension, B 12.131; their distress at Christ's ascension, B 12.135, Supp 7.39-43, Supp 10.139-46; at Mary's assumption, B 13.139-57, CHI 30.438-40; Peter the first, Paul the last, B 15.171; cast lots for ministries, B 19.229; chose deacons after the Ascension, CHI 3.44; preceded to heaven by St Stephen, CHI 3.50; their chastity, CHI 4.58, CHI 21.308, LS 10.202-10; left their wives to follow Christ, CHI 4.58, CHII 6.158-66; signified by shepherds CHI 7.106; not made kings, CHI 16.232; hold keys to heaven, CHI 26.370; Jewish persecution of, CHI 27.388,

CHI 28.402, CHII 24.1-6,
Supp 9.178-98; on the day of
judgement, CHI 27.394-96,
CHI 36.542, CHII 38.182-88,
Supp 4.126-31, Supp 11.354-64;
their individual qualities,
CHI 38.586; intercession by,
CHII 8.58-65; their mission signified
by bread, CHII 25.97-110; Christ's
friends, CHII 35.34-45; confessors
of Christ, CHII 38.192-212;
inherited Christ's power to heal,
LS 16.142-45; commissioning of,
LS 16.146-83; signified by light,
Supp 1.317-20; their exorcisms,
Supp 4.116-25; Jewish origins of,
Supp 5.194-204; reaped seed sown
by prophets and patriarchs,
Supp 5.247-64; Christ acted through,
Supp 6.324-27; signified by the
twelve hours of the day,
Supp 6.349-54; Christ predicted
their passions to them,
Supp 9.207-18; become learned men,
Supp 14.226-33; their poverty,
Supp 16.183-86; learned their faith
from the Creed, W 7.19-25.

ARCHITECTURE: *see also*
CHURCHES, THE TEMPLE OF
SOLOMON; the devil interferes with
the building of St Benedict's
monastery, CHII 11.187-204;
architects signify teachers,
CHII 36.23-26; men should uphold
each other like stones in a wall,
CHII 40.125-29; on the Day of
Judgement, men's works will be
tested like architects' constructions,

CHII 40.233-38; St Thomas builds
in India, LS 36.13-106; divine
architecture, LS 36.61-76, 125-44,
184-87; the Pentateuch signified by
five porticoes, Supp 2.59-67; the
believer should build himself as a
house pleasing to God, W 18.75-78.

THE ARK OF THE COVENANT:
see also THE JEWS, THE TEMPLE OF
SOLOMON; its sojourn among the
Philistines, Supp 21.210-81.

ARROW: *see also* BOW, WAR; the
devil's arrows of sin, V 4.308-21
(Vf 4.340-54).

THE ASCENSION: *see also*
CHRIST, PENTECOST; narrated, **B11**,
CHI 21, Supp 1.434-36,
Supp 7.31-43, Supp 8.219-27,
Supp 11.46-53, 519-25,
W 6.188-92, W 7.78-87; church on
the site of, B 11.125-29; Christ left
footprints at, B 11.125-27; apostles'
distress at, B 12.135, Supp 7.39-43,
Supp 10.139-46; Christ's eucharistic
prayer in St John's gospel
corresponds to, **CHII 22**; and
Rogationtide, Supp 11a.153-61.

ASCETICISM: *see also*
ABSTINENCE, THE BODY,
CASTRATION, CHASTITY,
CONTINENCE, FASTING, MARRIAGE,
MONKS, SAINTS, SEXUALITY, SIN, THE
SOUL; of John the Baptist, B 14.169,
CHI 25.352, 358, CHII 3.14-20,
LS 16.94-105; of St Benedict,

CHII 11.45-60; of St Martin,
CHII 34.120-32, V 18.279-83
(Vs 18.C113-C117); English rule
not as strict as elsewhere,
LS 13.106-109; of St Æthelthryth,
LS 20.31-40; opens up God's
secrets, LS 23B.19-55; of desert
monasteries, LS 23B.88-148; of
St Mary of Egypt, LS 23B.483-585;
of St Guthlac, V 23.5-12
(Vs 23.5-8).

ASH WEDNESDAY: *see also*
ASHES; traditions of, LS 12.16-20;
peril of refusing ashes on,
LS 12.41-58.

ASHES: *see also* ASH WEDNESDAY;
signify mortality, LS 12.16-20; and
repentance, LS 12.33-40.

ASS: *see also* ANIMALS;
law-abiding Jews likened to,
CHI 14.208; signifies humankind,
CHI 14.208.

ASSASSINATION: *see also*
MURDER, POISON; of Edward,
W 20BH.70-7[1], W 20C.82-83,
W 20EI.77-78.

THE ASSUMPTION OF MARY:
see also [appendix 2: MARY THE
MOTHER OF CHRIST] narrated, **B 13,
CHI 30, CHII 29;** uncertainty
about, CHI 30.438, 440,
CHII 29.115-33.

ASTROLOGY: *see also*

DIVINATION, FATE, THE MAGI,
SORCERY; angers God, CHI 6.100;
its invalidity, CHI 7.110-12,
LS 5.273-84; a machine for,
LS 5.250-70.

ASTRONOMY: *see* ASTROLOGY.

AUGURY: *see* ASTROLOGY,
DIVINATION, SORCERY.

B

BABEL: *see* THE TOWER OF BABEL
[appendix 2: BABYLON].

BAPTISM: *see also* CHRISTENING,
THE EPIPHANY, FORGIVENESS, THE
HOLY SPIRIT, SIN, WATER [appendix 1:
JOHN THE BAPTIST]; general
expositions, CHII 1.110-20,
Supp 12, W 8b.37-66, W 8c.1-28;
the devil tests men after, B 3.27-29;
of Christ, B 3.27-29, CHII 3.91-121,
Supp 1.437-54, Supp 11.12-19,
Supp 11a.81-93, V 16.1-69
(Vs 16.1-52); St Martin lived his
baptismal vows before taking them,
B 18.213, LS 31.51-57, V 18.32-43
(Vs 18.27-35); St Martin raises a
dead man to baptize him,
B 18.217-19, CHII 34.94-105,
LS 31.207-26, V 18.94-123
(Vs 18.75-C8); St Andrew baptizes
the Myrmedonians, B 19.245-47;
Christ replaced circumcision with
baptism, CHI 6.94-96; and
repentance, CHI 20.292; no one
should be baptized twice,

CHI 20.292, CHII 3.217-18,
224-28, Supp 12.78-94; delivers the
heathen from the devil to God,
CHI 21.304-306; drives out devils,
CHI 21.306, Supp 4.231-34;
signified by the passage of the Red
Sea, CHI 22.312, CHII 12.186-91;
John the Baptist's, CHI 25.352,
CHII 3.20-25, 50-60, 192-218; of
St Paul, CHI 27.390; the baptized
clothed with Christ, CHI 39.606; and
forgiveness, CHII 3.20-25; water
hallowed by Christ's, CHII 3.96-98;
opens heaven, CHII 3.108-14; its
efficacy, CHII 3.219-32,
Supp 12.91-94; vows of,
CHII 3.245-86, Supp 17.171-79,
W 13.22-31, W 15.33-36,
W 18.138-49; vicarious efficacy of
child baptism, CHII 3.246-72,
CHII 8.120-27, W 8c.126-38,
W 13.26-31; of Æthelbert of Kent,
CHII 9.216-25; signified by blood
and/or water from Christ's side,
CHII 14.321-23, V 1.259-65
(Vf 1.328-35); St Martin requests as
a child, CHII 34.7-11; of St Basil,
LS 3.67-80; angel refuses the
embrace of an unbaptized person,
LS 5.299-302; given to Cornelius by
St Peter, LS 10.109-71; martyrdom
automatically confers,
LS 11.293-98; and good works,
Supp 4.235-45; established in the
name of the Trinity, Supp 9.96-109;
unbaptized infants have the lightest
torment in hell, Supp 11.497-503;
unbaptized infants damned,
Supp 12.106-15; its effects invisible,

Supp 12.116-33; three dips into the
water signify the Trinity,
W 8b.45-47; not invalidated by the
failings of the celebrant,
W 8c.36-41; and the Holy Spirit,
W 18.78-90.

THE BEATITUDES: *see also* THE
BLESSED, SCRIPTURE, TEACHING,
VIRTUES; explicated, CHI 36.548-56.

BEES: *see also* ANIMALS; procreate
asexually, CHII 1.86-90; born of
rotting flesh, Supp 1.268-74.

BIRDS: *see also* ANIMALS, DOVE,
CORMORANT, EAGLE, PIGEON, RAVEN;
created from water, CHI 1.16;
signify teachers, CHI 35.522;
carrion birds signify the rapacious,
CHI 38.586; signify kinds of men,
CHII 3.182-91; signify devils,
CHII 6.70-78; signify pride,
LS 16.163.

BISHOPS: *see also* THE CHURCH,
EXCOMMUNICATION, MONKS,
PRIESTS; general expositions, **W 17**;
negligent, B 4.43-45, W 17.41-50;
their duties, B 4.45-49,
CHII 19.100-111, CHII 20.186-87,
W 15.1-8, 27-45, W 17.14-16,
36-39; power to forgive sins,
CHI 16.232-34; signified by
shepherds, CHI 17.238; wield
Peter's authority, CHI 26.370,
W 17.28-35; Augustine establishes
succession in England,
CHII 9.247-53; Cuthbert's career as,

CHII 10.226-323; should be chosen for virtue rather than ancestry, LS 10.222-31; should be cautious, LS 13.125; St Martin ordained against his will, LS 31.254-309; must not abandon churches, Supp 14.195-206; signified by farmers, Supp 18.153-68; respect for, Supp 20.274-303; corruption among, V 11.90-99 (Vs 11.73-79); and excommunication, W 14.53-62, W 15.1-8, 27-45; ordained by Christ, W 17.1-14; origin of office, W 17.16-35; people must follow their teaching, not their example, W 17.68-74.

BLASPHEMY: *see* APOSTASY, ERROR, HERESY, MURDER.

THE BLESSED: *see also* CHRISTIANS, THE DAMNED, HEAVEN, HELL, MAN, THE RIGHTEOUS, SALVATION, THE SINFUL; those who pay tithes, B 4.51; will replace the fallen angels, CHI 14.214, CHI 15.222, CHII 5.187-94; Christ will look different to the blessed and the damned on the day of judgement, CHI 15.222-24, V 2.15-19 (Vf 2.18-22); the grief of the damned part of their joy, CHI 23.332-34; will be like gods, CHI 26.366; on the Day of Judgement, CHI 27.396, Supp 11.343-46, 405-34, 451-59, V 4.117-93 (Vf 4.131-213); their number, CHII 5.187-94; desire the arrival of others in heaven, Supp 11.153-56; behold the torments

of the damned, Supp 11.261-67; will rule like angels, Supp 11.533-44; signified by eagles, Supp 18.210-16.

BLINDNESS: *see also* DISEASE, HEALING, LIGHT; general expositions, **B 2, CHI 10**; signifies the human condition, B 2.17, CHI 10.154; blind man prefers sight to wealth, B 2.21; of the devil, CHII 30.26-30; signifies unrighteousness, Supp 1.294-98; spiritual, Supp 2.76-77.

BLOOD: Christ's a red gem, B 1.9-11; contains the whole life of animals, CHI 1.16; signifies forgiveness, CHII 14.319-20; signifies baptism, V 1.259-65 (Vf 1.328-35); Christ bought us with, W 13.45-46.

BOASTING: *see* PRIDE, VAINGLORY.

THE BODY: *see also* ADULTERY, ASCETICISM, CASTRATION, DEATH, FASTING, THE FIVE SENSES, FORNICATION, THE FOUR ELEMENTS, GLUTTONY, HAND, RESURRECTION (GENERAL), SEXUALITY, THE SOUL; its relation to the soul: B 2.21, CHI 10.158-60, CHI 14.218, CHI 19.264, CHII 31.40-49, LS 1.176-225, LS 17.1-15, Supp 2.105-108, Supp 6.143-59, Supp 11.216-19, 243-60, 481-86, V 4.117-307 (Vf 4.131-339), V 7.94-108 (Vf 7.102-18), V 9.68-82 (Vs 9.54-64),

V 22.147-50 (Vs 22.117-19), 157-63 (125-29); sinners are the devil's limbs, B 3.33, CHI 11.168; rejoined with the soul on the Day of Judgement, B 5.57, CHI 20.294, V 4.162-83 (Vf 4.180-202); its mortality and corruption, B 5.57-59, B 8.99-101, B 10.111-13, CHI 1.16, CHI 7.118, CHI 28.410, V 2.56-60 (Vf 2.78-83), V 4.207-209 (Vf 4.230-32), 266 (294-95), V 9.101-106 (Vs 9.79-83), V 13.19-40 (Vs 13.17-33), V 21.207-10 (Vs 21.176-79), V 22.41-46 (Vs 22.33-37); God will reconstitute on the Day of Judgement, B 5.57, B 7.95, CHI 20.294, LS 20.109-12; of Mary, B 13.147-49; the darkness of, CHI 8.132; its desires signified by grass, CHI 12.188; a temple of God, CHI 14.210-12; of the risen Christ, CHI 16.230, 234, CHI 21.296, Supp 25c.1-19; Christians are Christ's limbs, CHI 19.260, 272, CHI 27.390, CHI 32.482, CHII 1.160-62, CHII 15.225-44, CHII 35.81-83, Supp 11.433-34, Supp 12.206-11, Supp 25c.1-19, W 8b.69-71, W 8c.100-101, W 10c.5-8, W 18.124-26; signifies the unity of the Church, CHI 19.272-74; mortification of, CHI 25.360, CHII 11.45-60, LS 17.60-66; the governing of, CHI 32.482; in old age, CHI 32.488-90, V 9.89-97 (Vs 9.70-76); a gateway for sin, CHI 33.492; not to be maimed,

CHI 34.516, Supp 19.61-65; and worldly cares, CHII 6.90-105; immortality after the general resurrection, CHII 31.55-56; citizens of Tours steal St Martin's, CHII 34.314-27; heaven is a foreign land to, CHII 38.38-44; the soul is to the body as God is to the soul, LS 1.141-46, 205-208; purity more than bodily, LS 9.84-93; virginity preserves the body from corruption after death, LS 20.107-112, LS 32.164-88; the wicked are Antichrist's limbs, Supp 18.386-90, W 1b.12-15; absolute sundering from soul after death, V 9.68-82 (Vs 9.53-64).

BOW: *see also* ARROW, WAR; the devil's bow of pride, V 4.308-21 (Vf 4.340-54).

BREAD: *see also* THE EUCHARIST; St Peter foils Simon Magus with blessed bread, B 15.177-79, CHI 26.376-78; signifies teaching, CHI 11.168, CHI 19.264-66, CHII 25.110-20, Supp 19.1-9; the miracle of the loaves and fish, **CHI 12, CHII 25**; five loaves signify the Pentateuch, CHI 12.186-88, CHII 25.19-34; signifies the Trinity, CHI 18.248; signifies love, CHI 18.250; Julian the Apostate scorns blessed bread, CHI 30.448-50, LS 3.205-227; St Cuthbert's miraculous loaves, CHII 10.51-73; in the eucharist, CHII 15.86-254, LS 3.153-68;

apostles recognize Christ in the breaking of, CHII 16.64-74; signifies Christ, CHII 16.186-99, V 5.116-24 (Vf 5.133-41); signifies gifts of the Spirit, CHII 25.64-71; signifies apostolic mission, CHII 25.97-110; 'Bethlehem' means 'house of bread', V 5.116-24 (Vf 5.133-41.

BREATH: Christians are Christ's, Supp 17.160-67.

C

CAMEL: *see also* ANIMALS; burdened camel signifies covetousness, CHII 40.195-99.

CANNIBALISM: among the Myrmedonians, B 19.229.

CASTRATION: *see also* ASCETICISM, THE BODY, SEXUALITY; forbidden, Supp 19.61-65.

CELIBACY: *see also* CHASTITY, CONTINENCE, MARRIAGE, SEXUALITY, WIDOWHOOD; of clergy, CHII 6.136-57, LS 10.222-31, LS 31.1066-1102, W 10a.33-36; celibates should not despise the married, Supp 30.8-15.

CHARITY: *see* ALMSGIVING, LOVE, POVERTY, TITHING, WEALTH.

CHASTITY: *see also* ABSTINENCE, ASCETICISM, CELIBACY, DIVORCE,

FORNICATION, MARRIAGE, SEXUALITY, VIRGINITY, WIDOWHOOD; of the apostles, CHI 4.58, CHII 6.158-66, LS 10.202-10; signified by myrrh, CHI 7.118; of Elijah, Enoch, and Christ, CHI 21.308; difficulty of, CHI 25.360; during Lent, CHII 7.21-37; signified by girded loins at Passover, CHII 15.303-306; wedded couples may separate for the sake of, CHII 19.166-69; the Holy Spirit promised to the chaste, LS 9.72-80; chastity of the will, LS 9.84-93; in marriage, LS 20.120-35.

CHILDREN: *see also* BAPTISM, CHRISTENING, THE HOLY INNOCENTS, PARENTHOOD; parent-child relationships, B 10.109, CHI 26.378, CHII 19.186-214, Supp 19.53-60; not responsible for their parents' sins, CHI 7.114; signify humility, CHI 9.138, CHI 34.512-14; St Paul's admonitions to; men God's children, CHI 19.258-60; example of children cursed by their mother, CHII 2.98-176; and baptismal vows, CHII 3.245-86, CHII 8.120-27; vicarious nature of infant baptism, CHII 3.262-72, CHII 8.120-27, W 8c.126-38; the devil appears to St Benedict in the form of a child, CHII 12.109-17; must mature, Supp 19.14-22; children dedicated to God's service by their parents ought not to demur, Supp 19.53-60; child sacrifice, Supp 21.565-71; collapse of family loyalties during last days, W 5.98-100, W 20BH.56-58, W 20C.69-71, 84-92, W20EI.61-63, 92-95; should be taught as soon as they can speak, W 8c.138-44; infants sold into slavery, W 20BH.41-42, W 20C.47-48, W 20EI.46-47.

THE CHOSEN: *see* THE BLESSED, CHRISTIANS, FAITH, THE RIGHTEOUS.

CHRIST: *see also* ANGELS, THE ANNUNCIATION, ANTICHRIST, THE ASCENSION, BAPTISM, CIRCUMCISION, CREATION, THE DAY OF JUDGEMENT, EASTER, THE EPIPHANY, THE EUCHARIST, GOD, THE HARROWING OF HELL, THE HOLY SPIRIT, THE INCARNATION, THE JEWS, THE LAW OF MOSES, THE NATIVITY, THE PASSION, PROPHECY, THE RESURRECTION OF CHRIST, TEMPTATION, THE TRANSFIGURATION, THE TRINITY; his humility, B 1.5, 11-13, B 2.23, B 6.65-67, B 8.103, B 9.105, CHI 2.32, 36, CHI 9.138, 40, CHI 11.168, 174, CHI 14.210, CHI 21.300, CHI 22.320, CHI 29.426, CHI 40.610, CHII 3.98-99, CHII 31.60-66, LS 16.113-29, V 5.1-6 (Vf 5.1-7), 184-90 (207-14), V 17.64-76 (Vs 17.51-60), W 6.160-71; lived on earth like an exulting giant, B 1.9; his blood a red gem, B 1.9-11; signified by gold, B 1.11, B 9.105; signified by light, B 2.17, B 9.105-107, CHI 2.36, CHI 9.144,

CHI 35.530, Supp 1.286-98, 321-25, Supp 6.343-48, LS 28.108-12, LS 29.14-16, V 17.121-23 (Vs 17.93-95); his human and divine natures, B 2.19, B 3.33-35, B 7.91, CHI 2.40, 42, CHI 4.68-70, CHI 7.106-108, CHI 7.116, CHI 8.120, CHI 9.136-38, CHI 9.150, CHI 10.156-58, CHI 14.216, CHI 16.230, CHI 21.296, CHI 21.300, CHI 23.336, CHI 38.578, CHI 39.600, CHII 12.267-73, CHII 13.137-49, CHII 15.273-92, CHII 22.39-49, 89-117, 172-79, CHII 23.142-46, CHII 24.99-115, CHII 29.24-29, LS 16.106-12, Supp 1.1-3, 17-26, 455-60, Supp 5.102-109, 225-39, Supp 7.44-51, 136-61, 189-94, 221-26, Supp 8.205-12, Supp 11.347-53, Supp 12.212-18, Supp 17.215-19, V 1E.90-99, V 1.111-15 (Vf 1.164-69), V 16.112-26 (Vs 16.87-98), W 6.134-53, 160-71, W 7.33-37; his poverty, B 2.23, CHI 9.140, CHI 10.160-62; suffered of his own free will, B 3.29-33, B 7.83-85, CHI 10.164, CHI 14.214, CHI 15.228, CHI 38.588, CHII 1.27-28, CHII 13.118-36, CHII 14.98-113, CHII 22.36-39, LS 24.147-51, Supp 3.130-32, Supp 10.204-10, V 1E.90-99, W 7.53-55; co-eternal with the Father, B 3.31, CHI 2.32, 40, CHI 13.198, CHI 20.278-80, CHII 1.8-11, CHII 13.205-20,

LS 31.749-74; signified by Solomon, CHII 40.74-93, W 18.66-67; burns the house of a widow who sought to seduce St Eugenia, LS 2.257-63; as lover and bridegroom, LS 2.352-66, LS 7.27-62; his epistle on healing, LS 24.81-123; signified by an angel, Supp 2.115-24; is the hand of God, Supp 4.150-51, 163-66; was a Jew, Supp 5.194-204; meaning of 'messiah' and 'Christ', Supp 5.205-10; allowed Lazarus to die, Supp 6.328-33; meaning of 'Jesus', Supp 8.59-62; his omniscience, Supp 8.242-49; summaries of his ministry, Supp 11a.102-27, V 21.87-96 (Vs 21.67-74), W 6.171-92, W 7.50-55; is the food of the angels, Supp 20.128-31; signified by manna, Supp 20.128-31; his omnipotence, V 1.111-15 (Vf 1.164-69); signified by Augustus, V 5.38-56 (43-65); as Son of God, V 16.127-38 (Vs 16.99-108); false Christs during the last days, W 2.37-42; childhood, W 6.164-69; his honesty contrasted with the perversity of Antichrist, W 9.129-49.

CHRISTENING: *see also* BAPTISM; St Martin asks for, B 18.211, CHII 34.7-11, LS 31.23-25; drives out devils, CHI 21.304, W 8b.14-19, W 8c.29-35; salt used during, W 8b.22-25, W 8c.53-56; use of the Creed during, W 8c.56-59; rites of, W 8c.56-71; three dips into the font signify the Trinity, W 8c.78-81.

CHRISTIANS: *see also* THE BLESSED, THE CHURCH, FAITH, MAN, THE RIGHTEOUS; duties of, B 4.47-49, CHI 6.96-98; signified by crowds following Christ, B 6.81, CHI 8.120; persecution of during last days, CHI pref.4-6, CHII 37.79-112, W 2.52-57; signified by sheep, **CHI 17**; are Christ's limbs, CHI 19.260, 272, CHI 27.390, CHI 32.482, CHII 1.160-62, CHII 15.225-44, CHII 35.81-83, Supp 11.433-34, Supp 12.206-11, Supp 25c.1-19, W 8b.69-71, W 8c.100-101, W 10c.5-8, W 18.124-26; signified by the Queen of Sheba, CHII 40.175-213; apostasy of early Christians, LS 5.21-60, Supp 14.140-46; signified by the name 'Israel', LS 16.29-35; will not be able to perform miracles during the last days, LS 35.346-60, Supp 18.356-65, W 3.48-49, W 5.58-64; signified by a ship, Supp 14.75-84; are the breath of Christ, Supp 17.160-67; signified by animals at the Nativity, V 5.139-50 (Vf 5.156-68); contemporary heathen conduct themselves better than, W 20BH.22-32, W 20C.28-38, W 20EI.27-37.

THE CHURCH: *see also* BISHOPS, CHRISTIANS, CHURCHES, FAITH, MONKS, PRIESTS; signified by Martha, B 6.73; signified by Mary, Martha's sister, B 6.73; comprises men both better and worse, B 6.75,

CHI 35.526, 536, CHII 24.173-88, CHII 39.32-33; signified by Bethpage, B 6.77; Peter its shepherd, B 15.171; Paul its teacher, B 15.171; signified by Rachel weeping, CHI 5.84; its unity, CHI 9.142, CHI 19.272-74, CHI 26.368, CHII 15.237-44, CHII 40.110-17, Supp 2.125-29; built on a rock, CHI 26.368; its purity, CHI 33.492; is Christ's bride and the mother of Christians, CHI 33.494, CHI 35.520, CHII 1.91-109, CHII 4.29-36, CHII 12.312-17, CHII 39.87-92, Supp 6.192-95, Supp 12.130-33, W 10c.41-54; signified by Noah's ark, CHI 35.536; signified by Eve, CHII 4.100-104, CHII 14.323-27; is the kingdom of heaven, CHII 5.36-39, CHII 39.25-32, Supp 4.173-82; signified by the tent of the tabernacle, CHII 12.334-43; signified by a ship, CHII 24.131-39; signified by a rock, CHII 24.162-72; signified by the wise and foolish virgins, CHII 39.32-96; is a virgin, CHII 39.81-87; signified by Solomon's temple, **CHII 40**, W 18.67-69, 91-123; believers its stones, CHII 40.108-10; gentiles in the Church signified by the Samaritan woman at the well, Supp 5.113-17; began at the Pentecost, Supp 10.95-104; its holy days, Supp 11.1-90, Supp 11a.75-196; feebleness of the English church, Supp 14.98-107, W 20BH.22-37, 43-47, 59-60, 73-75, W 20C.28-44, 54-57, 71-73, 84-87, W20 EI.27-42, 64-65, 176-84; signified by a field, Supp 18.146-52; signified by Christ's manger, V 5.139-50 (Vf 5.156-68); to be honoured, W 10c.39-54; its taxes, W 13.70-79.

CHURCHES: *see also* THE CHURCH; regular attendance enjoined, B 4.47; the church of St Michael, **B 17, CHI 34**; consecration of, CHI 34.506, **W 18**; underwater church where St Clement was drowned, CHI 37.564-66; of St Stephen, CHII 2.8-47, 56-70; attendance at, CHII 29.110-15, W 14.18-20; selling of, CHII 40.293-98, LS 19.248-54; proper conduct in, LS 13.68-86, V 20.5-15 (Vs 20.4-12), W 18.37-65; priests and bishops should not abandon, Supp 14.195-206; pillaging of, V 11.90-99 (Vs 11.73-79), V 15.19-21 (Vs 15.15-17), W 10c.51-54, W 20BH.22-28, 33-37, 73-75, W 20C.39-44, 84-87, W 20EI.37-42, 80-83; attendance at mass during Lent, W 14.18-20.

CIRCUMCISION: *see also* THE JEWS; Christ's, **CHI 6**; Jewish practice explained, CHI 6.90-92; Christ replaced with baptism, CHI 6.94-96; of the spirit, CHI 6.94-96; Christ's signifies the general resurrection, CHII 4.277-93.

CLOTHING: St Martin's heals, B 18.223, CHII 34.213-16, 264-66; animal skins signify mortality, CHI 1.18; St John the Evangelist's heals, CHI 4.72-74; symbolizes good works, CHI 14.210; signifies joy, CHI 15.222, CHI 21.298-300; vanity of splendid clothing, CHI 23.328-30, V 2.98-103 (Vf 2.128-33), W 11.125-32: signifies love, CHI 35.528; symbolizes virtue, CHI 39.606; St Gregory's luxurious dress, CHII 9.38-42; virtue and good works clothe the righteous, V 21.57-61 (Vs 21.45-48).

CLERGY: *see* BISHOPS, CHURCHES, MONKS, PRIESTS, TEACHING.

COINS: *see also* WEALTH; Roman, LS 23.474-88.

CONFESSION: *see also* FORGIVENESS, REPENTANCE, SIN; general expositions, V 3.17-42 (Vf 3.19-47), V 8.9-26 (Vf 8.10-29), V 10.248-56 (Vs 10.186-92); unconfessed sins the devil's wealth, B 4.43; inward confession alone insufficient, CHI 8.124; its difficulty, CHI 10.156; exhortation to, CHI 10.164, CHI 39.604; unconfessed sins signified by Lazarus' grave wrappings, CHI 16.234; before taking the eucharist, CHI 19.266; and repentance, CHI 19.268; signified by the secrets spoken by the Queen of Sheba to Solomon, CHII 40.193-95; not to be deferred, LS 12.167-77; honesty in, LS 12.177-253; and the Last Judgement, Supp 16.94-98; unconfessed sins must be atoned for, V 8.27-32 (Vf 8.30-36).

CONTEMPLATIVE LIFE: *see also* ACTIVE LIFE, MONKS, PRAYER; wild animals do not harm contemplatives, CHI 6.102, CHI 32.486-88, CHII 33.175-88, LS 4.399-407, LS 23B.761-95, LS 24.40-57, LS 30.413-20, LS 35.253-306, LS 37.231-49; signified by Mary, the sister of Martha, CHII 29.36-109; will never have an end, CHII 29.54-70; signified by the pair in bed on the world's last night, Supp 18.90-109.

CONTINENCE: *see also* ABSTINENCE, ASCETICISM, THE BODY, CHASTITY, CLOTHING, GLUTTONY, SEXUALITY; signified by myrrh, CHI 7.118; its difficulty, CHI 25.360; during Lent, CHII 7.21-37; symbolized by girded loins at Passover, CHII 15.303-306; the mother of all virtues, LS 1.155-67; in enjoying God's liberality, LS 11.356-61.

CONVERSION: *see also* FAITH, THE HEATHEN, THE JEWS; general expositions, CHI 27.398, **Supp 17**; of Nero's wife, B 15.173; of Saul/Paul, CHI 3.52, CHI 27.386, 390; of philosophers, CHI 4.60-62;

late conversion, CHII 5.122-42; of the good thief, CHII 5.129-42; of England, CHII 9.1-11, 81-88, 164-253; of Constantine, CHII 18.1-37, LS 7.260-86, Supp 26.7-15; of saints' torturers, LS 4.175-80, 213-39, LS 11.195-217, LS 19.98-106, LS 22.159-90, LS 29.301-12, LS 34.214-65, LS 35.194-218; conversion of the heathen signified by Peter's fishing, Supp 14.108-14; convert signified by a ship, Supp 14.176-86.

CORMORANT: *see also* ANIMALS, BIRDS; signifies devils, CHII 34.275-82, LS 31.1309-27, V 18.230-42 (Vs 18.152-61).

COUNSEL: good counsel a gift of the Spirit, CHI 22.322, CHII 25.64-71, Supp 9.139-49, W 9.35-37; Isaiah's condemnation of false counsellors, W 11.150-55.

COVETOUSNESS: *see also* GLUTTONY, SIN, WEALTH, THE WORLD; general expositions, CHI 4.64-66, CHI 27.398, CHII 12.505-10, V 20.89-97 (Vs 20.70-76), W 10c.71-79; of Judas, B 6.69; part of Adam's temptation, CHI 11.176, W 10c.78-79; part of the temptation of Christ, CHI 11.176-78; source of all evil, CHI 18.256; caused the ruin of the Jerusalem temple, CHI 28.406; signified by carrion

birds, CHI 38.586; in the decalogue, CHII 12.328-33; slavery to wealth, CHII 31.24-40; signified by burdened camel, CHII 40.195-99; like hell, LS 16.280-85; consequences of, V 20.93-96 (Vs 20.73-75); remedied by fear of God, love, and mercy, V 20.96-97 (Vs 20.75-76); signified by dropsy, V 20.91-93 (Vs 20.71-73); Isaiah's condemnation of, W 11.118-24, 133-39.

CREATION: *see also* ANIMALS, THE FALL OF ADAM AND EVE, THE FALL OF THE ANGELS, THE TRINITY; narrations and general expositions, CHI 1.8-16, CHII 1.6-13, CHII 12.273-99, Supp 11a.44-52, Supp 21.12-44, V 19.12-31 (Vs 19.10-26), W 6.21-33; the earth's beauty in its first age, B 10.115, LS 16.232-36, W 3.27-29; man created to replace fallen angels, B 11.121-23, CHI 1.12, CHI 2.32, CHI 13.192, CHI 14.214, CHI 15.222, CHI 24.342-44, CHII 5.183-94, W 6.34-39; and the Trinity, CHI 1.10, CHI 13.192, CHI 20.278, CHI 26.366-68, LS 1.14-19, 33-35, LS 15.1-8, Supp 1.84-97, Supp 21.12-27; creatures cannot be greater than their Creator, CHI 1.10; God did not create evil, CHI 1.12; of Adam, CHI 1.12, 16, CHI 16.236, V 19.23-29 (Vs 19.19-23), W 6.34-39, W 15.8-18; of Eve, CHI 1.14, V 19.29-31 (Vs 19.34-36), W 6.34-39; man is

the work of God's hands, CHI 1.16,
CHI 13.192, V 8.46-48
(Vf 8.51-53); Christ the Creator,
CHI 7.104, LS 30.59-65,
Supp 1.70-76, 167-82,
Supp 6.111-28, Supp 9.62-63; all
creation acknowledges Christ as the
Creator, CHI 7.108, CHI 11.172,
CHI 15.228, CHII 14.287-89,
LS 11.171-76, 340-43,
LS 25.176-79, V 1.235-39
(Vf 1.300-305), V 16.69-98
(Vs 16.53-75), W 12.25-34;
distinction between Creator and
created, CHI 20.278; creation wars
on sinful humankind, CHII 37.52-65,
W 3.29-44; the three dimensions of,
CHII 40.202-205; the time before
not to be inquired into, LS 1.19-25;
humans assist in, LS 11.308-11;
God's constant renewal of,
Supp 2.220-46, Supp 25b.1-4; the
created world reveals the Creator,
Supp 20.411-15; creature's
obligations to the Creator,
V 22.129-56 (Vs 22.103-24).

THE CREED: *see also* FAITH, THE
LORD'S PRAYER THE MAGNIFICAT;
general expositions, **W 7a**,
W 8c.144-55; Peter's, B 15.187;
effects miraculous healing,
LS 5.357-61; its purpose,
LS 12.261-63; teachers must teach
the meaning of, LS 12.264-67; to be
said before a journey, LS 17.96-99;
and the Lord's Prayer, W 7.8-18;
apostles learned their faith from,
W 7.19-25; baptizands must learn,

W 8c.15-18; at christenings,
W 8c.56-59; and opposition to the
devil, W8c.116-26.

CRIME: *see* ASSASSINATION,
MURDER, POISON, PROSTITUTION,
THIEVES

THE CROSS: *see also* THE
HARROWING OF HELL, THE PASSION,
RELICS; terrifies devils in hell,
B 4.47; the sign of, B 4.47,
LS 17.145-47, LS 21.469-78,
LS 23b.676-85, 722-24,
LS 27.147-56, LS 31.366-426,
719-21; erected in hell, B 7.87;
appears on the day of judgement,
B 7.91, Supp 11.290-91, V 2.7-8
(Vf 2.8-9), V 15.92-112
(Vs 15.73-88), V 21.165-66
(Vs 21.127-28), W 2.65-69;
protection of, B 19.243,
CHII 33.86-109, LS 23b.761-88;
St Andrew preaches mystery of,
CHI 38.588-90; signified by lamb's
blood on Passover, CHII 15.52-59;
Constantine's vision of,
CHII 18.11-22; invention of,
CHII 18.38-53, LS 27.4-13;
St Martin goes to battle armed with,
CHII 34.45-58; Oswald raises a
cross before battle, LS 26.14-29;
feasts of, LS 27.14-19, 137-42; its
capture and abuse by the heathen,
LS 27.20-85; miracles associated
with, LS 27.82-133.

CROWNS: *see also* KINGS;
'Stephen' means 'crowned',

CHI 3.50; of martyrdom,
LS 34.72-77, 110-16.

THE CRUCIFIXION: *see* CHRIST,
THE, CROSS, EASTER, THE
HARROWING OF HELL, THE PASSION,
THE RESURRECTION, TORTURE.

CURSING: *see also* OATHS; of
animals, CHI 6.100-102; none
should curse Adam and Eve,
CHI 7.114; children cursed by their
mother, CHII 2.98-176; forbidden,
CHII 2.190-216; harms him who
curses, CHII 2.203-205; usurps
God's authority to judge,
CHII 2.210-15; church plunderers
cursed, W 10c.51-54.

D

DAMNATION: *see* THE DAMNED,
THE DAY OF JUDGEMENT, HELL, SIN,
THE SINFUL.

THE DAMNED: *see also* DESPAIR,
THE DEVIL, DEVILS, HELL, SIN, THE
SINFUL; those who refuse to pay
tithes, B 4.49; Christ will appear
different to the damned and the
blessed on the day of judgement,
CHI 15.222, CHI 21.300,
Supp 11.347-353, V 2.15-19
(Vf 2.18-22); left behind at the
harrowing of hell, CHI 15.228; the
blessed in heaven observe their
suffering, CHI 23.332-34; on the day
of judgement, CHI 27.396,
Supp 11.343-53, 435-59, 466-72,

V 2.15-19 (Vf 2.18-22), V 8.44-87
(Vf 8.48-96), V 15.172-99
(Vs 15.135-55); live in peace for the
present, CHI 28.408; damnation
signified by the sack of Jerusalem,
CHI 28.408-10; devils torment,
CHI 28.410, CHII 21.34-54; Mary
and other saints retrieve a portion of
on the day of judgement,
CHII 39.184-92, V 15.142-99
(Vs 15.111-55); no intercession for,
CHII 39.192-98; St Basil annuls a
contract with the devil,
LS 3.358-461; narration of the
judgement of a damned soul,
V 4.194-307 (Vf 4.214-339); lament
of a lost soul, V 22.47-56
(Vs 22.38-45); haggle with devils
for relief of their torments,
V 22.56-66 (Vs 22.46-54).

DANCE: female dancers sent to
tempt St Benedict's monks,
CHII 11.153-70.

DARKNESS: *see also* DAY, LIGHT,
NIGHT; the shadows of sin,
B 2.17-19; of the body, CHI 8.132;
of the mind, CHI 8.132; hell's fires
dark, CHI 8.132, CHI 35.532,
CHII 21.34-39; of the world, B 2.17,
CHI 18.248; inner and outer,
CHI 35.530; signifies philosophy,
LS 35.16-23.

DAY: *see also* DARKNESS, DAYS OF
THE WEEK, LIGHT, NIGHT; signifies
Christ, CHI 2.36, CHI 39.604,
Supp 6.343-48; eternal life one

the Jews during, V 8.39-42
(Vf 8.44-47); will come on account
of the world's sins, W 3.7-9.

DAYS OF THE WEEK: *see also*
DAY, TIME; origin of names of,
Supp 21.166-80.

DEAFNESS: signifies those who
won't listen to Christ's commands,
Supp 2.80-81.

DEATH: *see also* THE BODY, THE
FALL OF ADAM AND EVE, HEAVEN,
HELL, SIN, THE SINFUL, SUICIDE;
general expositions, **V 9 (Vs 9)**,
V 13 (Vs 13); overcome by Christ's
death, B 3.33; the body's corruption
after, B 5.57-59, B 8.99-101,
B 10.111-13, CHI 1.16, CHI 7.118,
CHI 28.410, V 2.56-60
(Vf 2.78-83), V 4.207-209
(Vf 4.230-32), 266 (294-95),
V 9.101-106 (Vs 9.79-83),
V 13.19-32 (Vs 13.17-27),
V 21.207-10 (Vs 21.176-79),
V 22.41-46, (Vs 22.33-37); the dry
bones speak, B 10.113, V 13.19-32
(Vs 13.17-27); men must anticipate,
B 5.61, CHII 39.205-17; all will rise
again, regardless of the manner of
their deaths, B 7.95,
Supp 11.332-38, V 21.172-74
(Vs 21.132-34); none can escape,
B 10.109, CHI 21.306-308,
CHI 39.602, Supp 6.143-59,
V 1.115-17 (Vf 1.169-71),
V 4.13-16 (Vf 4.15-18), 65-67
(74-77), V 9.41-58 (Vs 9.33-46),

V 14.62-77 (Vs 14.51-61); its
suddenness, B 11.125; of Mary,
B 13.137-47; worldly pleasures
become griefs after, B 16.195;
signified by animal skins, CHI 1.18;
need never have come to be,
CHI 1.18; and original sin,
CHI 1.18, V 21.126-29
(Vs 21.97-101); signified by myrrh,
CHI 7.116; Christ's death signified
the life of mortal men, CHI 15.224;
devils assail the soul during,
CHI 28.414, CHII 20.57-92,
111-51, Supp 11.164-76,
Supp 27.15-47, 83-105,
V 18.290-99 (Vs 18.C122-127);
signifies sin, CHI 33.492; of the
soul, CHI 33.496, CHII 20.180-83,
Supp 6.160-212, Supp 11.118-38;
not feared by the faithful,
CHI 38.590, Supp 11.205-207; a
change for the better,
CHII 13.150-68; signified by
vinegar, CHII 14.222-27; Fursey's
return from, CHII 20.39-56,
199-251; angels attend the souls of
the dying, CHII 20.39-92, 152-55,
Supp 11.181-84; Drihthelm's return
from, **CHII 21**; likened to sleep,
CHII 39.92-104; equated with sin,
Supp 6.137-42; God did not create,
Supp 11.107-10; kinds of,
Supp 11.111-17, V 9.32-37
(Vs 9.26-30); the pain of sometimes
confers forgiveness,
Supp 11.200-204; the dead cannot be
raised by sorcery, Supp 29.50-65,
118-23; berated by damned soul for
having delayed, V 4.221-22

(Vf 4.244-45), 248-49 (274-75); soul's deeds revealed at, V 9.59-65 (Vs 9.47-52); a foretaste of hell, V 9.97-101 (Vs 9.76-79); contemplation of, V 22.113-28 (Vs 22.90-102).

THE DECALOGUE: *see* THE JEWS, THE LAW OF MOSES, [appendix 1: MOSES].

DECEIT: *see also* APOSTASY, ERROR, HERESY, SLANDER, TEACHING; prevalence of, B 5.55, W 5.22-23; character of, B 5.55; of Antichrist, CHI pref.4-6, W 4.43-52, 79-83; the devil summons false fire from heaven, CHI pref.6, CHII 30.90-129, W 4.62-66; the devil deceived Adam and Eve, CHI 1.18-20, CHI 13.192, 194, CHI 18.252, CHI 31.460, CHII 30.125-29, V 14.17-23 (Vs 14.15-19), W 7.37-38, W 12.12-13; mutual deception of Herod and the Magi, CHI 7.118-20; signified by a serpent, CHI 18.252; lying in the decalogue, CHII 12.326-28; of physical desire, LS 2.163-67; will be exposed on the day of judgement, LS 19.172-77; contemporary admiration for, W 21.23-26.

DEER: *see* ANIMALS, HART.

DEMONS: *see* DEVILS, THE DEVIL, EXORCISM, HELL.

DESIRE: *see also* COVETOUSNESS, GLUTTONY, SEXUALITY; earthly desires symbolized by grass, CHII 25.72-78; its proper function to lead us to eternal things, LS 1.100-103; part of the soul's resemblance to the Trinity, LS 1.112-22, LS 34.164-70; kills the soul if it rules, LS 1.146-48; deceit of, LS 2.163-67; an oppressive law, V 2N.144-46; cooled by contemplation of death, V 22.111-14 (Vs 22.88-91); destructive, V 22.165-74 (Vs 22.131-38).

DESPAIR: *see also* THE DAMNED, HOPE; general expositions, CHII 12.514-19, 554-55, Supp 6.284-93, Supp 9.172-77, V 20.114-24 (Vs 20.90-97); good and bad, CHII 12.517-19, LS 16.293-94, V 20.114-20 (Vs 20.90-95); and repentance, CHII 19.54-59; the devil prompts, Supp 6.278-91; leads to eternal death, Supp 6.313-17; prompted by a vision of hell, Supp 19.208-41; and hope, Supp 19.242-54; consequences of, V 20.121-23 (Vs 20.95-96); remedied by rejoicing and hope of heaven, V 20.123-24 (Vs 20.96-97); St Guthlac wounded with poison of, V 23.13-29 (Vs 23.9-20).

THE DEVIL: *see also* ANTICHRIST, DECEIT, DEVILS, ERROR, EVIL, THE FALL OF ADAM AND EVE, THE FALL OF THE ANGELS, THE HARROWING OF HELL, HELL, IDOLATRY, SIN; tests men

after baptism, B 3.27-29,
CHI 11.170; quotes scripture falsely,
B 3.29; signified by Goliath, B 3.31;
the sinful are his limbs, B 3.33,
CHI 11.168, 172; perceived only
Christ's human nature, B 3.33;
unconfessed sins are his wealth,
B 4.43; forfeits his claim to fallen
humankind and/or the damned,
B 7.85-87, CHI 1.26, CHI 14.216,
CHI 20.292, Supp 10.197-203; his
pride, B 13.159, CHI pref.6,
CHI 1.10, 14, CHI 9.138; Antichrist
man and devil, CHI pref.4,
W 4.6-11; cannot heal, CHI pref.4,
Supp 4.86-89; source of lies,
CHI pref.4, CHI 11.170; source of
evil, CHI pref.4, CHI 1.12,
CHI 11.170, Supp 1.183-95,
W 8c.173-74; his hatred and envy of
humankind, CHI 1.16-18,
LS 37.80-87, Supp 11.107-10,
V 19.37-48 (Vs 19.31-39),
W 6.39-44; cannot create,
CHI 6.100-102; signified by Herod
ordering the massacre of the
innocents, CHI 7.108-110; permitted
to test Christ, CHI 11.166-68,
Supp 10.188-203; his uncertainty
over Christ's identity, CHI 11.168,
176; instigates but cannot compel
evil acts, CHI 11.170,
CHII 13.42-65; 'devil' means
'falling down', CHI 11.172; the
prince of worldly men, CHI 11.172;
sent another devil to tempt Eve,
CHI 13.194; instigated Christ's
passion, CHI 14.216; signified by a
greedy fish, CHI 14.216; signified

by a wolf, CHI 17.238-40,
Supp 4.206-209; driven out by
christening, CHI 24.304,
W 8b.14-19, W 8c.29-35; desires
worship, CHI 31.460; signified by
night, CHI 39.604; assaults monks,
CHII 11.109-17, 187-204, 434-42;
signified by Pharaoh,
CHII 12.178-91; men become his
children through imitation,
CHII 13.70-80; a sower of discord,
CHII 19.81-85; in the book of Job,
CHII 30.26-37, 90-129;
impersonates Christ,
CHII 34.229-38, LS 31.749-74;
pacts with, LS 3.358-461; urges on
persecutors of early Christians,
LS 11.131-39, LS 16.197-202,
LS 29.183-97, LS 37.10-20; prayer
destroys his weapons, LS 13.50-54;
seeks to disrupt prayer, LS 13.55-59;
tests Job's patience, LS 16.39-54;
instigated heresy, LS 16.203-205;
his rage at impending end of the
world, LS 16.225-27; corrupted
Saul, the king of Israel, LS 18.8-11;
and criminals, LS 19.188-93;
St Martin offers him a chance to
repent, LS 31.726-48; prompts
despair, Supp 6.278-91; prince of
this world, Supp 7.171-80; equated
with hell, Supp 11.459-65; possesses
partial foreknowledge,
Supp 29.97-104; described as a
dragon, V 4.46-48 (Vf 4.52-53);
stakes a claim to the damned,
V 4.295-302 (Vf 4.328-33),
V 10.63-100 (Vs 10.48-76); the
meaning of 'Lucifer', V 19.12-17

(Vs 19.10-14); pleased by misbehaviour in church, V 20.5-15 (Vs 20.4-12), W 18.47-65; to be released after a one-thousand-year imprisonment, W 5.40-46; opposed by the Creed, W 8c.116-26; his seven evil gifts, W 9.56-106; signified by a werewolf, W 16b.35; has led England astray, W 20BH.6-9, W 20C.12-15, W 20EI.11-14.

DEVILS: *see also* THE DEVIL, THE FALL OF THE ANGELS, HELL, IDOLATRY; are terrified by the cross, B 4.47; at the harrowing of hell, B 7.85-87; seize damned souls on the day of judgement, B 7.93-95; abet sorcery, B 15.173-75, 189, CHI 26.380, CHII 27.38-81, LS 3.358-461; and the spread of idolatry, CHI 1.22-24, Supp 21.190-201; a devil dispatched to tempt Eve, CHI 13.194; believe in God, CHI 21.304; signified by the Roman besiegers of Jerusalem, CHI 28.410, CHII 21.34-54; torment the damned, CHI 28.410; assail souls at death, CHI 28.414, CHII 20.57-92, 111-51, Supp 11.164-76, Supp 27.15-47, 83-105; V 18.290-99 (Vs 18.C122-C127); cause disease, CHI 31.454, W 6.82-95; impersonate heathen gods and animate their idols, CHI 31.454-70, CHI 38.588, CHII 33.7-40, LS 2.39-40, LS 8.59-61, LS 14.16-22, LS 29.46-50,

LS 34.117-25, Supp 21.190-201, 282-91, V 12.1-11 (Vs 12.1-9), W 12.1-21; possession by proportional to a person's sins, CHI 31.460; exiled to wastelands, CHI 31.464; appearance of, CHI 31.466, LS 4.282-98; signified by birds, CHII 6.70-78; St Cuthbert inhabits a devil-haunted island, CHII 10.158-76; acknowledge Christ, CHII 23.177-85, Supp 17.297-305; signified by cormorants, CHII 34.275-82, LS 31.1309-27, V 18.230-42 (Vs 18.152-61); their powers explained by an angel, LS 6.324-35; allowed to test men with torments, LS 17.196-201, W 6.79-95; repelled by patience, LS 17.205-12; expelled by baptism, Supp 4.231-34; show a sick thegn the record of his good deeds and sins, Supp 19.136-207; retain vestiges of their angelic powers, Supp 29.97-104; impersonate angels, Supp 29.105-10; war with angels on the Saturday preceding the day of judgement, V 15.129-37 (Vs 15.102-108); damned souls plead with for relief, V 22.56-66 (Vs 22.46-54); assail St Guthlac, **V 23, (Vs 23).**

DIRECTION: *see* EAST, LEFT, NORTH, RIGHT, WEST.

DISEASE: *see also* BLINDNESS, DEAFNESS, EXORCISM, THE FALL OF ADAM AND EVE, LAMENESS, LEPROSY, SUFFERING; human existence like a disease, B 5.59; part of the human condition, B 5.59-61; plagues during the last days, B 10.107-109; devil cannot heal unless he has first inflicted, CHI pref.4; inflicted by God, CHI pref.4, CHI 31.470, LS 13.139-46, 240-74, LS 31.1277-99; caused by devils, CHI 31.454, W 6.82-95; occasion for miracles, CHI 31.474; promotes humility, CHI 31.474, LS 20.49-60; plague preceding St Gregory's papacy, CHII 9.89-93, 109-22, 156-63; ten plagues of Egypt, CHII 12.55-80, Supp 1.225-50; God loves those he afflicts with illness, CHII 19.246-51; St Peter desires his daughter's paralysis, LS 10.232-48; a consequence of and punishment for sin, LS 13.139-46, LS 20.49-60, Supp 2.276-86, V 22.83-88 (Vs 22.67-71), 95-99 (77-81); the sick signify the Jews, Supp 2.68-75; sickbed repentance, Supp 11.195-99; God the remedy for all ills, V 4.174-79 (Vf 4.196-98); dropsy signifies covetousness, V 20.91-93 (Vs 20.71-73); signifies contemporary tribulations, W 20BH.18-22, W 20C.24-26, W 20EI.23-25.

DIVINATION: *see also* ASTROLOGY, FATE, PROPHECY, SORCERY; angers God, CHI 6.100, LS 17.88-91; casting lots permissible if done in faith, LS 17.84-87; from the devil, LS 17.100-107.

DIVINITY: *see* CHRIST, GOD, THE HOLY SPIRIT, THE TRINITY.

DIVORCE: *see also* ADULTERY, MARRIAGE, SEXUALITY, WIDOWHOOD; a couple may separate for a vow of chastity, CHII 19.166-69; Christ's prohibition on, Supp 19.34-41; barren wives not to be abandoned, Supp 19.105-11.

DOG: *see also* ANIMALS, FOX, WOLF; their licks heal wounds, CHI 23.330; signify vicarious efficacy of baptism, CHII 3.262-72; signify the heathen, CHII 8.88-98, 104-10; signify the Jews, CHII 8.88-98; devour Jezebel, LS 18.344-56; signify sinners, Supp 13.228-32; signify teachers, Supp 18.175-79, W 16b.28-26; the hundred-headed hound of hell, V 9.214-20 (Vs 9.134-39).

DOOMSDAY: see THE DAY OF JUDGEMENT, THE LAST DAYS.

DOVE: *see also* ANIMALS, BIRDS, PIGEON; general expositions, CHII 3.158-61, 172-73, 179-91, V 16.112-26 (Vs 16.87-98); signifies awe, CHI 9.140; signifies purity, CHI 9.142; its innocence and meekness, CHI 22.320, CHI 30.444, CHI 38.584, Supp 16.225-57, V 17.77-82 (Vs 17.61-65); St Peter

called the son of a dove,
CHI 26.368; sellers of doves signify
those who teach for gain,
CHI 28.412; miraculous dove
accompanies St Basil, LS 3.68-131;

DOUBT: *see also* DESPAIR, FAITH,
HOPE; the apostles' CHI 16.234,
CHI 21.300-302; and faith,
CHII 24.189-212.

DRAGON: evil women likened to,
CHI 32.486; confronts false monk,
CHI 35.534-36; St Philip defeats,
CHII 17.1-25; of wizards,
CHII 32.106-10; devil appears as,
Supp 11.168-76; wouldn't have
dared to harm Adam prior to his fall,
Supp 21.45-48; Daniel destroys,
Supp 21.432-93; on the day of
judgement, V 2.45 (Vf 2.59); devil
identified with, V 4.46-48
(Vf 4.52-53); flee from a cave where
the holy family shelter, V 6.63-68
(Vf 6.71-77).

DREAMS: varied provenance of,
LS 21.403-13.

DRUNKENNESS: *see also*
GLUTTONY; general exposition,
CHI 39.604; at funerals,
LS 21.307-17; Isaiah's
condemnation of, W 11.140-49;
avoidance of during Lent,
W 14.23-25.

DROPSY: *see* DISEASE.

E

THE EARTH: *see also*
AGRICULTURE, ANIMALS,
EARTHQUAKE, THE FLOOD, FLOWERS,
LIGHTNING, STORMS, THE WORLD;
belongs to God alone, B 4.51; at the
Creation, B 10.115, LS 16.232-36,
W 3.27-29; acknowledged Christ,
CHI 7.108, CHI 15.228, V 16.81-82
(Vs 16.61-62); its transformation
after the day of judgement,
CHI 40.616-18, Supp 11.508-18;
Fursey's vision of, CHII 20.93-103;
animated by wisdom,
Supp 1.275-79; God's control of
natural phenomena, Supp 13.43-47;
renewed by fire on the day of
judgement, Supp 18.81-85; worship
of, Supp 21.89, W 12.24; a middle
ground between heaven and hell,
V 4.72-77 (Vf 4.82-87).

EARTHQUAKE: *see also* EARTH;
warns against the removal of the
bodies of St Peter and St Paul from
Rome, B 15.193, CHI 26.384; a sign
that the earth acknowledged Christ
as its Creator, CHI 7.108,
CHI 15.228, V 16.81-82
(Vs 16.61-62); sent to help
Christians in war, CHI 34.504-506;
on the day of judgement, V 2N 6-7.

EAST: *see also* NORTH, WEST;
signifies youth, CHI 8.130; prayer
directed to, CHI 19.262.

EASTER: *see also* CHRIST, THE HARROWING OF HELL, THE PASSION, THE RESURRECTION; narrations and general expositions, **B 7, CHI 15, CHII 15, CHII 16,** Supp 11a.142-52; signifies the world to come, B 3.35.

ECLIPSE: *see* MOON, SUN.

EGGS: Christ's divinity and humanity like white and yolk of, CHI 2.40; signify hope, CHI 18.250.

ELEPHANT: *see also* ANIMALS; their nature, LS 25.564-73; in warfare, LS 25.551-86.

EMPERORS: *see* KINGS [appendix 1: AUGUSTUS, AURELIUS, CONSTANTINE, DECIUS, DOMITIAN, HELENA, JULIAN THE APOSTATE, MAXENTIUS, MAXIMUS, NERO, NERVA, THEODOSIUS, TIBERIUS, TITUS, TRAJAN, VALENS, VALENTINIAN, VESPASIAN].

ENVY: *see also* COVETOUSNESS, SIN; general expositions, CHI 39.604-606; a kind of murder, B 5.65; the devil's, CHI 1.16-18, CHI 39.606, LS 37.80-87, Supp 11.107-10, V 19.37-48 (Vs 19.31-39).

THE EPIPHANY: *see also* CHRIST, BAPTISM; narrations and general expositions, **CHI 7, CHII 3,** Supp 11a.86-93; **V 16 (Vs 16).**

ERROR: *see also* APOSTASY, DECEIT, HERESY, TEACHING; in England, CHI pref.2; saving another from saves one's self, CHII 19.281-84.

THE EUCHARIST: *see also* BREAD, CHRIST; general expositions, **CHII 15, V 14.65-85** (Vs 14.53-68), W 8b.67-71, W 8c.96-99; signified by Bethlehem, CHI 2.34; is Christ's body, CHI 2.34; spiritual bread, CHI 19.266; its virtues, CHI 19.266; confession before receiving, CHI 19.266; corpses of the excommunicated cannot abide, CHII 11.334-61; puts corpse of boy at rest, CHII 11.362-75; signified by manna, CHII 12.206-14; and the last supper CHII 14.63-68; signified by the eating of the Passover lamb, CHII 15.59-63; transubstantiation of, CHII 15.86-173, LS 3.153-68; apostles recognized Christ in the breaking of the bread, CHII 16.64-73; Christ administers to St Basil, LS 3.109-31; a Jew's curiosity about, LS 3.153-68; celebrants of must be celibate, LS 10.222-31; for the dying, Supp 11.177-80; should be taken more often, Supp 19.119-30; feast days on which it ought to be taken, Supp 19.119-30; for the sick, Supp 19.131-241; Christ more than food to Christians, Supp 20.134-39; heaven opens to the voice of a celebrant priest, V 14.77-85

(Vs 14.62-68); not invalidated by the sins of the celebrant, W 8c.36-41; is harmful if taken by the sinful, W 8c.45-52.

EVIL: *see also* THE CREATION, DEATH, THE DEVIL, DEVILS, FREE WILL, HELL, SIN, SUFFERING, TORTURE; God did not create, CHI 1.12, Supp 1.183-95; men not compelled to by fate, CHI 7.110-12; nothing good established unless evil first thrown down, CHI 9.144; devil can instigate but not compel, CHI 11.170; caused by covetousness, CHI 18.256; wicked deeds signified by stones of fallen temple, CHI 28.410; toleration of, CHI 35.526-28; caused by devils, Supp 11a.40-43; Christians must reject, W 10c.55-71.

EXCOMMUNICATION: *see also* BISHOPS, EXILE; general expositions, W 14.36-62, W 15; corpses of the excommunicated men leave their tombs at the elevation of the eucharist, CHII 11.334-61; wilfully excessive fasting subject to, LS 12.3-7; of Theodosius I by Ambrose, Supp 26.28-139; like Adam's fall, W 14.36-40.

EXILE: *see also* THE FALL OF ADAM AND EVE, EXCOMMUNICATION; of St John the Evangelist, CHI 4.58-60; of St Clement, CHI 37.560-66; Christ's incarnation a form of, CHII 38.38-44; excommunication a

form of, **W 15**; of Æthelræd, W 20BH.71.

THE EXODUS: *see* THE JEWS, THE LAW OF MOSES, MANNA, PASSOVER, [appendix 1: AARON, JOSHUA, MOSES].

EXORCISM: *see also* THE DEVIL, DEVILS, HEALING; by christening, CHI 24.304, W 8b.14-19, W 8c.29-35; its nature, CHI 31.460; Christ and the Gadarene demoniac, CHII 23.147-94, LS 17.190-98; considered the humbler office by St Martin, LS 31.139-44; of animals, LS 31.1038-55; signifies purification of repentant sinners, Supp 4.56-71; one devil will not cast out another, Supp 4.106-19; by the apostles, Supp 4.120-23.

F

FAITH: *see also* THE BLESSED, CHRISTIANS, THE CHURCH, CONVERSION, GOOD WORKS; general expositions, **CHI 20, V 19 (Vs 19)**, **W 10c**, W 13.1-11, W 18.134-37; the true faith, B 10.111; essential to good works, B 10.111, CHI 16.236; of the centurion in the gospels, CHI 8.126; the faithful signified by Israel, CHI 13.204; signified by a fish, CHI 18.250; piety a gift of the spirit, CHI 22.322, CHII 25.64-71, Supp 9.139-49, W 9.45-48; signified by a rock, CHI 26.368; disbelief signified by sleep, CHI 39.602; good works must accompany,

CHII 16.39-73; and doubt, CHII 24.189-212; cost of belief, CHII 34.79-85; God's gift, CHII 35.84-87; virginity of, CHII 39.78-81; signified by gold, CHII 40.181-87, 238-43; the faithful signified by clean animals, LS 25.55-60; belief in Christ signified by light, Supp 1.286-98; and faithlessness, Supp 7.85-89; and hope and love, V 3.1-13 (Vf 3.1-14); self-knowledge essential to, W 13.6-11; right practice of, W 13.63-84.

THE FAITHFUL: *see* THE BLESSED, FAITH.

THE FALL OF ADAM AND EVE: *see also* DEATH, THE DEVIL, DISEASE, EVIL, THE FALL OF THE ANGELS, MERCY, SIN; narrations and general expositions, CHI 1.12-20, CHI 13.192, 194, CHI 18.254, Supp 11a.47-52, V 16.177-84 (Vs 16.139-44), V 19.31-48 (Vs 19.27-39), W 6.44-52, W 15.8-23; Mary reversed, B 1.3-5, CHI 30.446; as exile, B 2.23, CHI 7.118, CHI 10.162, CHI 18.248, Supp 1.219-21, V 11.46-62 (Vs 11.38-51), V 14.17-20 (Vs 14.15-17), W 14.36-40, W 15.18-23; consequences of, B 2.17, CHI 1.18, CHI 7.112, CHI 9.144, CHI 10.154, CHII 1.110-18, LS 12.21-28, Supp 17.135-48, Supp 21.33-65,

V 21.126-29 (Vs 21.97-100); result of pride, B 2.23-25, CHII 31.78-84, V 2.93-95 (Vf 2.122-25); Eden became the wilderness of Christ's temptation, B 3.29; its effects reversed at the Ascension, B 11.123; Satan's envy of Adam and Eve, CHI 1.16-18, LS 37.80-87; God's mercy towards Adam and Eve, CHI 1.18-20, CHI 13.192, CHII 1.18-27, Supp 11a.53-61; the devil deceived Adam and Eve, CHI 1.18-20, CHI 13.192, 194, CHI 18.252, CHI 31.460, CHII 30.125-29, V 14.17-33 (Vs 14.15-27), W 7.37-38, W 12.12-13; we must return to paradise by a different route than that by which we left, CHI 7.118, V 16.184-97 (Vs 16.144-54); Adam tempted three ways, CHI 11.176-78; Adam fell through covetousness, CHI 11.176-78, W 10c.78-79; Adam's curse signified by Christ's crown of thorns, CHII 14.213-18, CHII 26.42-47; labour part of Adam's curse, CHII 31.38-40; Adam's lost beauty signified by flowers, CHII 31.67-74; the soul lost its blessedness but not its immortality, LS 1.150-53; Adam fell through contempt of God, LS 13.182-184; the origin of evil, Supp 1.183-89; signified by deaf and dumb man, Supp 17.85-98; Adam's pre-lapsarian beatitude, Supp 21.33-44; and fasting, V 3.101-19 (Vf 3.111-30).

FEAR: fear of God a gift of the spirit, CHII 25.70, Supp 9.143, W 9.48-51; fear of God the beginning of wisdom, CHI 36.550; and love, CHII 35.45-48; fear of fire a cure for fornication, V 20.86-88 (Vs 20.68-69), V 22.106-13 (Vs 22.85-90); fear of God a cure for covetousness, V 20.96-97 (Vs 20.75-76).

FIRE: *see also* THE DAY OF JUDGEMENT, FURNACE, HELL; St Martin saves a house from, B 18.221, CHII 34.161-83; the devil's false fire from the heavens, CHI pref.6, CHII 30.90-129, W 4.62-66; analogy for relationship between Christ and the Father, CHI 20.278; symbol of Christ's divinity, CHI 21.296; signifies love, CHI 22.320, CHI 24.344, CHI 36.540; signifies the Holy Spirit, CHI 22.320-26, CHII 3.163-78, CHII 15.280-84; symbol of God, CHI 22.322; on the day of judgement, CHI 40.616, CHII 40.232-38, 250-58, Supp 11.296, 302-303, Supp 18.75-85, V 2.1-5 (Vf 2.1-5), V 21.160-64 (Vs 21.122-25); illusory, CHII 10.113-26; Christ on the day of judgement likened to, CHII 12.195-205; waits at the world's periphery to purify souls, CHII 20.93-110; St Martin's hair flames as he celebrates the mass, CHII 34.241-43; at St Basil's baptism, LS 3.67-80; from heaven, LS 18.97-141, 240-55; miraculous fire ignites the throne of an Arian emperor, LS 31.650-81; destroys the enemies of Moses and Aaron, Supp 20.261-73; worship of Supp 21.87, W 12.22-23; analogy for the Trinity, V 16.153-62 (Vs 16.120-27); fear of a remedy for fornication, V 20.86-88 (Vs 20.68-69), V 22.106-13 (Vs 22.85-90); signifies contemporary tribulations, W 20BH.17-22, W 20C.24-26, W 20EI.23-25.

FISH: *see also* ANIMALS, BIRDS, FISHERMEN; created from water, CHI 1.10; miracle of loaves and, **CHI 12, CHII 25**; two fish signify the psalms and the prophets, CHI 12.188; greedy fish signifies the devil, CHI 14.216; signifies faith, CHI 18.250; fish escaped from St Peter's net signify the sinful, CHII 16.163-67, Supp 14.126-39; signifies Christ, CHII 16.186-99; signifies Christians, Supp 14.147-75.

FISHERMEN: *see also* FISH, THE SEA, SHIP; Christ chose fishermen before emperors, CHI 32.578; signify teachers, Supp 14.66-74; St Peter's fishing signifies evangelization of the heathen, Supp 14.108-114.

FLATTERY: among the sinful, CHI 33.492-94; its effects, CHI 33.494; signified by oil to be

bought by foolish virgins,
CHII 39.155-71.

THE FIVE SENSES: *see also* THE
BODY; general exposition,
LS 1.196-200; signified by five
monetary units, CHI 9.138,
CHII 38.44-49, 138-41; gateways of
sin, CHI 33.492; sight and the soul,
CHI 38.584; symbolized by oxen,
CHII 23.43-62; signified by the wise
and foolish virgins, CHII 39.34-40;
and virginity, CHII 39.40-47; ruled
by the soul, LS 1.195-96, 200-205.

THE FLESH: *see* THE BODY.

THE FLOOD: narrations and
general expositions, CHI 1.20-22,
CHII 4.111-28, W 6.56-69; Noah's
ark signifies the Church,
CHI 35.536; caused by fornication,
LS 13.185-89; the day of judgement
likened to, W 3.7-9.

FLOWERS: *see also* HERBS, LILY,
ROSE; Christ the golden blossom,
B 9; flowers from St Stephen's
church effect a miraculous
conversion, CHII 2.22-47; signify
Adam's lost beauty, CHII 31.67-74;
transfigured body of the blessed
likened to, V 4.157-58
(Vf 4.175-76).

FORGIVENESS: *see also*
CONFESSION, HEALING, REPENTANCE,
SIN; general expositions, **Supp 13,**

Supp 15, V 14.121-35
(Vs 14.96-107), W 7.93-95;
examples of, CHI 3.52,
LS 3.169-200, 527-63, 633-63; of
enemies, CHI 3.52-56,
Supp 13.103-105, Supp 15.80-89;
bishop's power of, CHI 16.232-34;
apostles' power of, CHI 16.232-34;
signified by the loosening of
Lazarus' grave garments,
CHI 16.234; mutual,
CHI 19.266-68; by the Holy Spirit,
CHI 22.322; not conferred by John
the Baptist, CHII 3.23-24; a species
of alms, CHII 7.38-46; signified by
blood, CHII 14.319-20; men must
forgive in order to be forgiven,
LS 12.254-60; Christ's forgiveness
signified by Augustus' general
amnesty, V 5.66-69 (Vf 5.78-82),
V 6.48-54 (Vf 6.54-60); conferred
on those who hear and speak the
gospels, V 10.1-8 (Vs 10.1-7);
signified by the heavens' opening at
Christ's baptism, V 16.100-11
(Vs 16.77-86); absolution during
Rogationtide, V 19.81-88
(Vs 19.65-71); almsgiving effects,
V 21.32-47 (Vs 21.26-37).

FORNICATION: *see also*
ADULTERY, THE BODY, CHASTITY,
DIVORCE, MARRIAGE, INCEST,
SEXUALITY, WOMAN; general
expositions, CHII 12.500-505,
549-53, V 20.82-88 (Vs 20.65-69);
a deacon miraculously cleared of
accusation of, CHII 33.156-69;
caused Noah's flood, LS 13.185-89;

caused the destruction of Sodom and Gomorrah, LS 13.190-215; of St Mary of Egypt, LS 23b.318-419; consequences of, V 20.83-86 (Vs 20.65-68); remedied by fear of fire, V 20.86-88 (Vs 20.68-69), V 22.106-13 (Vs 22.85-90).

FORTITUDE: *see also* PATIENCE, VIRTUES; a gift of the spirit, CHII 25.64-71, Supp 9.139-49, W 9.34-35; a virtue of the soul, LS 1.155-67; perseverance in hardship, V 11.21-45 (Vs 11.18-37), 70-86 (59-69), V 13.1-10 (Vs 13.1-9).

THE FOUR ELEMENTS: the human body composed of, B 3.35.

FOX: *see also* ANIMALS; signifies cunning, LS 16.160-62.

FREE WILL: *see also* EVIL, FATE, OBEDIENCE, SIN; of the angels, CHI 1.12, CHI 7.110-12; of Adam and Eve, CHI 1.18; of humankind, CHI 7.110-12, CHI 11.170, CHI 14.210, 212, LS 1.171-74, 253-71, W 7.74-78; of the Jews, CHI 14.216; causes soul to resemble the Trinity, CHI 20.283-90; purity a function of, LS 9.84-93; and fate, LS 17.222-71; signified by owner's departure from vineyard, Supp 3.106-14; a test, Supp 10.49-56.

FRUIT: *see also* AGRICULTURE,

HERBS; signify good works, CHII 26.47-100, CHII 35.96-97, LS 4.240-48.

FURNACE: *see also* FIRE; the Hebrew youths in, CHI 37.570, CHII 1.230-66, Supp 21.292-99.

G

THE GARDEN OF EDEN: *see* CREATION, THE FALL OF ADAM AND EVE.

GEMS: *see also* GOLD, SILVER, WEALTH; general expositions, CHI 4.60-62, 64, 68; Christ's blood a red gem, B 1.9-11; signify good works and virtues, CHII 40.181-87, 238-41; transfigured body of the blessed likened to, V 4.159-60 (Vf 4.177-78).

GIANTS: Christ like a giant, B 1.9; and the Tower of Babel, CHI 22.318; worship of, CHI 26.366, Supp 21.99-103; Goliath, LS 18.18-27; Judas Maccabeus likened to, LS 25.279-80; Hercules, LS 35.112-16; Moses' scouts report in the promised land, Supp 20.140-69.

GIFTS OF THE SPIRIT: *see* THE HOLY SPIRIT.

GLUTTONY: *see also* THE BODY, COVETOUSNESS, FASTING, SIN;

general expositions, CHI 39.604,
CHII 12.493-500, 548-49,
V 7.84-118 (Vf 7.91-129),
V 20.70-81 (Vs 20.56-64); how
Adam was tempted, CHI 11.176,
CHII 12.499-500, V 20.71-73
(Vs 20.57-58); how Christ was
tempted, CHI 11.176-78; damned
soul expostulates on to body,
V 4.248-56 (Vf 4.274-83);
consequences of, V 20.77-80
(Vs 20.62-64); remedied by
abstinence, V 20.80-81 (Vs 20.64);
Isaiah's condemnation of,
W 11.140-49.

GOD: *see also* CHRIST, THE
CREATION, THE HOLY SPIRIT, THE
TRINITY; omniscience of, B 2.19-21,
CHI 7.112-14, CHI 10.158,
CHI 20.288, CHI 39.604,
LS 1.41-44, 136-41, LS 17.253-65;
the source of all goodness, B 3.29,
B 4.39-41, CHI 7.114, CHI 17.238,
CHI 18.254, LS 1.89-92,
LS 11.312-16; patience of, B 3.33,
CHI 19.268-70, CHI 40.610,
LS 23b.384-91, Supp 15.39-54;
eternity of, CHI 1.8-10,
CHI 20.274-76, LS 1.47-49, 61-69;
omnipotence of, CHI 1.8-10,
LS 1.44-47, V 5.149-97
(Vf 5.220-22); unfathomability of,
CHI 1.10; created the world through
his wisdom, CHI 1.10; mercy of,
CHI 1.18-20, CHI 4.68,
CHI 13.192, CHI 7.112,
CHI 14.210, CHII 1.18-27,
CHII 5.210-33, CHII 19.47-54,

Supp 13.72-85, V 1E.1-7;
omnipresence of, CHI 8.126,
CHI 10.158, CHI 19.260-62,
CHI 20.286-88, CHI 24.348,
CHII 40.144-47, LS 1.136-41,
Supp 3.108-109, Supp 5.185-89;
tempts no one, CHI 19.268; signified
by fire, CHI 22.322; Simon Magus
claims to be, CHI 26.376; permits
suffering, CHI 31.472-74,
CHI 37.566, CHII 37.202-205,
LS 17.174-212, V 22.89-95
(Vs 22.72-76), W 3.65-73; covenant
with Abraham, CHII 12.17-27; men
become children of through
imitation, CHII 13.70-80; loving
God men love themselves,
CHII 19.43-47; soul is to the body as
God is to the soul, LS 1.141-46,
205-208; signified by rich man in
parable, Supp 16.39-48; addresses a
blessed soul on the day of judgement,
V 4.162-66 (Vf 4.180-84); addresses
the damned on the day of judgement,
V 8.44-87 (Vf 8.48-96); relations
with humankind, V 21.4-9
(Vs 21.4-7); conceals power during
reign of Antichrist, W 3.45-48,
W 5.64-66.

THE GODS: *see* IDOLATRY.

GOLD: *see also* GEMS, SILVER,
WEALTH; signifies Christ, B 1.11;
symbolizes wisdom, CHI 7.116;
signifies royalty, CHI 7.116-18,
V 5.57-66 (Vf 5.67-77), V 6.33-47
(Vf 6.37-52); martyrs tried like gold,
CHI 36.544; signifies faith,

46

H

HAND: God holds world in his,
CHI 1.10-12, CHI 13.198; God
created Adam by hand, CHI 1.16,
CHI 13.192, V 8.46-48
(Vf 8.51-53); signifies Christ's
human nature, CHI 8.122; signifies
Christ's power, CHI 8.122; signifies
God's power, CHI 14.212; held back
from evil by the fear of God,
CHI 35.530; lack of mercy signified
by withered hand, Supp 2.82-90;
Christ is God's hand,
Supp 4.150-51, 163-66.

HARP: *see* MUSIC, POETRY.

THE HARROWING OF HELL:
see also THE CROSS, THE DEVIL,
DEVILS, HELL, THE PASSION, THE
RESURRECTION; narrations and
general expositions, B 6.67, **B7**,
B 8.103, CHI 1.26-28, CHI 14.216,
CHI 15.224-26, CHI 31.462,
Supp 4.191-96, Supp 11a.142-52,
V 1.287-99 (Vf 1.360-71),
W 7.65-68, W 15.23-26; the devil
forfeited his right to the damned,
CHI 14.216, Supp 10.197-203; John
the Baptist at, CHI 25.364,
CHI 32.480.

HART: *see also* ANIMALS;
miraculous hart appears to
St Eustace, LS 30.16-53, 102-10.

HATE: *see also* MURDER, WAR,
WRATH; a kind of murder, B 5.63-65.

HEALING: *see also* CHRIST,
CONFESSION, DEATH, DISEASE,
FORGIVENESS, MIRACLES, RELICS,
SAINTS; spiritual medicine, B 8.97,
B 10.107, CHI 8.124-26,
CHI 31.472, CHI 33.496-98,
LS 22.36-127, **V 20**; the devil heals
falsely, CHI pref.4, CHI 31.462-64,
W 4.53-62; by St Peter's shadow,
CHI 22.316, LS 10.19-22; dogs'
licks heal wounds, CHI 23.330;
Christ the physician, CHI 24.338;
Elisha refuses to perform for money,
CHI 27.400; should be sought from
God, CHI 31.470; cures sometimes
harsh, CHI 31.472; spells for,
CHI 31.474-76; Jewish medicine
unavailing, CHII 2.80-97,
LS 3.566-628; mercy is medicine for
sin, CHII 7.46-51; St Martin healed
animals, CHII 34.259-61; teaching is
symbolic healing, CHII 38.232-41;
at baptism, LS 5.144-51; power to
heal not to be sold, LS 5.182-205; by
the Lord's Prayer and the Creed,
LS 5.357-61; apostles inherited
Christ's power of, LS 16.142-45;
sorcerers should not be consulted for,
LS 17.122-28; medicine must be
accompanied by prayer,
LS 17.213-21; Christ's epistle on,
LS 24.81-123; St Martin heals by
letter, LS 31.574-84; healing of sin
more important than healing bodies,
Supp 2.98-104, 134-38; symbolism

of Christ's, Supp 2.184-210; St Luke was both a spiritual and an ordinary physician, Supp 13.1-7.

THE HEATHEN: *see also* CONVERSION, THE DEVIL, DEVILS, IDOLATRY, VIKINGS; general exposition, **Supp 21**; make war on Christians, B 17.201-203, CHI 34.504-506, LS 24.1-27, LS 26.7-29, 150-63, LS 32.26-163; all nations except Israel were heathen before Christ, CHI 14.206-208; on the day of judgement, CHI 27.396; Supp 11.384-90; V 8.39-42 (Vf 8.44-46); pagan prophecies of Christ, CHII 1.214-66, Supp 1.113-44; signified by vineyard workers, CHII 5.77-87; signified by a dog, CHII 8.88-98, 104-10; the heathen soul signified by madness, CHII 8.30-34; signified by the good thief at the crucifixion, CHII 14.257-62; signified by those summoned to a feast, CHII 23.95-110; signified by partakers of the miracle of the loaves and fish, CHII 25.46-63; ignorance of eternal life, LS 5.61-68; signified by unclean beasts, LS 10.96-106; receive the Holy Spirit, LS 10.151-71; now will not be excused, LS 11.344-47; worship devils, Supp 5.118-22, Supp 11.384-90, Supp 21.72-81, 197-201; Jewish exclusivism towards, Supp 5.123-29; Rome was heathen in Christ's time, V 1.99-100

(Vf 1.151-52); conduct themselves better than contemporary Christians, W 20BH.22-32, W 20C.28-38, W 20EI.27-37; contemporary slavery to, W 20BH.75-81, W 20C.87-92, W 20EI.83-85.

HEAVEN: *see also* ANGELS, THE BLESSED, THE HEAVENS, SALVATION; the joys of, B 2.25, B 5.65, B 8.103-105, CHI 16.238, CHI 19.270-72, CHI 21.296, CHI 23.334, CHI 35.526, CHII 40.208-17, LS 5.81-85, LS 12.88-96, Supp 2.109-14, Supp 11.320-25, 548-71, Supp 25a.1-20, V 2.112-19 (Vf 2.144-51), V 5.197-204 (Vf 5.223-30), V 8.90-94 (Vf 8.99-104), V 9.168-209 (Vs 9.99-129), V 10.263-75 (Vs 10.196-205), V 14.141-47 (Vs 14.112-16), V 15.200-206 (Vs 15.156-60), V 19.170-78 (Vs 19.133-39), V 20.197-203 (Vs 20.110-14), V 21.238-55 (Vs 21.201-15), W 7.151-53; becomes visible on the day of judgement, B 7.91-93; signified by mountains, CHI 8.120, CHII 24.92-99, 131-39; the true homeland, CHI 10.162; narrow path to, CHI 10.162; visions of, CHI 27.392, CHII 20.155-71, CHII 21.55-69, 83-91, LS 36.125-44; equality of reward in, CHI 30.446; opened by baptism, CHII 3.108-14; 'alleluia' its song, CHII 5.272-87; the fellowship of,

CHII 35.105-108; a foreign land to the flesh, CHII 38.38-44; heathen ignorance of, LS 5.61-68; eternal life is one unending day, LS 12.79-81; signified by the seashore, Supp 14.63-65; signified by the promised land, Supp 20.376-89; God's might more exalted than, V 5.194-96 (Vf 5.218-21); opens to the voice of a priest celebrating the eucharist, V 14.77-85 (Vs 14.62-68); desire for a cure for sloth, V 20.110-13 (Vs 20.87-89); hope of a cure for despair, V 20.123-24 (Vs 20.96-97).

THE HEAVENS: *see also* HEAVEN, THE MOON, THE STARS, THE SUN; during the last days, B 7.91-93, CHI 4.610, W 5.105-108; acknowledged Christ as their creator, CHI 7.108, CHI 15.228, CHI 21.298, V 16.72-75 (Vs 16.55-57); signify God, CHI 19.262; their transformation after the day of judgement, CHI 40.616-18, Supp 11.508-18; God allowed them to retain their original splendour after the fall of Adam and Eve, Supp 1.206-208; God governs, Supp 7.178-80; heavenly bodies named for false gods, Supp 21.181-89; heavens' opening at Christ's baptism signifies forgiveness, V 16.100-11 (Vs 16.77-86).

HELL: *see also* DAMNATION, DARKNESS, THE DEVIL, DEVILS, FIRE,

THE HARROWING OF HELL; slack priests and bishops in, B 4.43-45; the horrors of, B 5.61-63, B 17.209-11, CHI 4.68, CHI 8.132, LS 4.380-88, LS 5.74-79, LS 7.137-40, LS 17.29-34, Supp 11.326-31, 466-92, V 2.60-68 (Vf 2.84-93), V 4.51-56 (Vf 4.58-64), V 8.75-87 (Vf 8.83-96), V 9.20-31 (Vs 9.17-25), 84-143 (66-E15), V 9L.151-63, V 21.211-18 (Vs 21.180-86), V 22.37-46 (Vs 22.30-37), 56-66 (46-54), W 3.65-73, W 7.122-28, W 13.84-92; no one need go to after Christ, B 7.103, CHII 5.160-68, W 6.158-60, W 13.32-36; visions of, B 17.209-11, CHII 21.34-54, 80-83, V 23.118-52 (Vs 23.93-119); created by God for rebel angels, CHI 1.12; signified by infant Christ's manger, CHI 2.34; acknowledged Christ as the creator, CHI 7.108, CHI 15.228, V 16.88-90 (Vs 16.67-68); its fire dark, CHI 8.132, CHI 35.532, CHII 21.34-39; the broad path to, CHI 10.162-64; heresy the gate to, CHI 26.368; the righteous inhabitants of before the harrowing, CHII 5.143-60; equated with the devil, Supp 11.459-65; suffering in proportional to sin, Supp 11.493-96; sight of prompts despair, Supp 19.208-41; five likenesses of in this life, V 9.84-113 (Vs 9.65-87), impossibility of describing its terrors and pains, V 9.108-30 (Vs 9.84-E5);

solitude in, V 9.136-43
(Vs 9.E9-E15).

HERBS: *see also* AGRICULTURE,
FLOWERS, MYRRH, TREES; medicinal,
CHI 31.476, Supp 1.216; signify
repentance, CHII 15.269-72.

HERESY: *see also* APOSTASY,
ERROR, IDOLATRY; Antichrist's,
CHI pref.4; varieties of,
CHI 7.116-18, CHI 20.290,
LS 16.208-11; the Arian heresy,
CHI 20.290, CHII 34.86-90,
LS 16.206-207, LS 31.184-95,
650-81, Supp 10.159-69; is the
gateway to hell, CHI 26.368;
punishment of, CHI 26.370;
concerning the Assumption of Mary,
CHI 30.436-438; concerning the
head of John the Baptist,
CHI 32.486; foretold by Christ,
CHII 26.14-19; heretical accounts of
Mary and other saints saving a
portion of the damned from hell,
CHII 39.184-92; denying Christ's
co-eternity, LS 1.5-9; heretical
advisors of the emperor Valens,
LS 3.312-17; heretical churches
under Valens, LS 3.318-23; St Basil
defeats heretics in a contest of
prayer, LS 3.324-54; instigated by
the devil, LS 16.203-205; denial of
resurrection and judgement,
LS 23.353-93; that Judas will be
forgiven, LS 27.157-64; during
St Martin's time, LS 31.831-41; the
Manichean heresy, Supp 1.410-26;
denying Christ's humanity,
Supp 4.276-81; repentance of
heretics, Supp 6.221-27; of
Olympius, Supp 10.170-76.

HOLY DAYS: *see* CHRISTMAS, THE
CHURCH, EASTER, PASSOVER, THE
SABBATH.

THE HOLY INNOCENTS:
narrations and general expositions,
CHI 5, V 6.59-63 (Vf 6.66-71); the
mothers of the Holy Innocents are
also martyrs, CHI 5.84.

THE HOLY SPIRIT: *see also*
CHRIST, GOD, PENTECOST, THE
TRINITY; the comforter, B 12.131,
135-37, CHI 16.232, Supp 7.39-42,
Supp 10.80-104; likened to the wind,
B 12.133, Supp 12.150-64; like a
dove, B 12.135, CHII 3.150-63,
V 16.112-126 (Vs 16.87-98); is the
love and will of the Father and the
Son, CHI 1.10, CHI 13.196,
CHI 15.228, CHI 20.280,
CHI 22.324, CHI 33.498-500,
LS 1.35-38, Supp 6.234-57,
Supp 7.208-14, Supp 10.92-94,
Supp 11a.11-13, 210, 221;
quickened God's creation to life,
CHI 1.10, CHI 2.40; spoke through
St Stephen, CHI 3.44; not Christ's
father, CHI 13.196; at Christ's
resurrection, CHI 16.232; forgives
sin, CHI 22.322, CHI 33.498; gifts
of, CHI 22.322, CHII 16-200-207,
CHII 25.64-71, 121-29,

Supp 5.210-13, Supp 9.114-23, 139-49, Supp 11a.183-85, Supp 17.120-29, **W 9**; inspired David, CHI 22.322; inspired the apostles, CHI 22.322; likened to fire, CHI 22.320-26, CHII 3.163-78, CHII 15.280-84; signified by water, CHI 25.362, Supp 5.131-58; marvelled at the manner of Mary's death, CHI 30.442-44; the unforgivable sin against, CHI 33.498-500, Supp 6.217-27, 269-77; at Christ's baptism, CHII 3.134-61; at the Pentecost, CHII 3.163-78; is God's finger, CHII 12.240-50, Supp 4.132-72, Supp 17.120-29; promised to the pure, LS 9.72-80; defeated pharaoh's sorcerers, Supp 4.139-44; inscribed the tables of the law, Supp 4.145-49; pities the penitent, Supp 6.276-77; inspired the Old Testament prophets, Supp 7.67-72; came to the entire world, Supp 7.73-84; glorified Christ's human nature, Supp 7.221-26; brought knowledge of the Trinity, Supp 9.89-95; role in the Immaculate Conception, V 10.16-18 (Vs 10.13-15); at baptism, W 18.78-90.

HOMOSEXUALITY: *see* SEXUALITY.

HONESTY: general expositions, **B 5**; in confession, LS 12.177-253; Christ's contrasted with Antichrist's

perversity, W 9.129-49; monastic, W 10a.45-48.

HONEY: *see also* BEES; bees breed from, CHII 1.86-90; signifies Christ, CHII 16.192-99; signifies spiritual reading, V 19.79-80 (Vs 19.63-64).

HOPE: *see also* DESPAIR, FAITH; signified by eggs, CHI 18.250; and despair, Supp 19.242-54; and faith and love, V 3.1-13 (Vf 3.1-14).

HORSE: *see also* ANIMALS; St Paul's fall from signifies his humbling, CHI 27.390.

HOSPITALITY: toward strangers, CHII 16.73-97; toward others and God, CHII 19.36-47.

HUMILITY: *see also* PRIDE; general expositions, **CHI 8**, CHI 34.512, CHII 5.169-204, **CHII 28**, V 2.90-96 (Vf 2.118-25), V 21.10-18 (Vs 21.8-14); of Christ, B 1.5, 11-13, B 2.23, B 6.65-67, B 8.103, B 9.105, CHI 2.32, 36, CHI 9.138, 140, CHI 11.166, 174, CHI 14.210, CHI 21.300, CHI 22.320, CHI 29.424-26, CHI 40.610, CHII 3.98-99, CHII 31.60-66, LS 16.113-29, V 5.1-6 (Vf 5.1-7), 184-91 (207-14), V 16.48-56 (Vs 16.36-42), V 17.64-76 (Vs 17.51-60); necessity of, B 8.99, St Michael's, B 17.197, St Martin's,

B 18.215, CHII 34.110-20,
LS 31.88-89, 137-44; a condition of
Adam's blessedness, CHI 1.14; of a
centurion, CHI 8.126-28, 132-34;
signified by children, CHI 9.138,
CHI 34.512; of Mary, CHI 13.200;
remedy for pride, CHI 22.318,
V 20.68-69 (Vs 20.55); signified by
valleys, CHI 25.362, Supp 5.178-79;
signified by St Paul's fall from his
horse, CHI 27.390; disease can
promote, CHI 31.474; of the poor in
spirit, CHI 36.548-50; the humble
live in heaven on earth, CHI 36.550;
God chose the humble first,
CHI 38.578; signified by a dove,
CHI 38.584; of John the Baptist,
CHII 3.99-101, V 16.48-56
(Vs 16.36-42), incomplete without
obedience, CHII 3.101-107;
St Gregory's CHII 9.89-108;
St Gregory enjoins upon
St Augustine of Canterbury,
CHII 9.238-46; St Cuthbert's,
CHII 10.158-70, 226-38; saves the
sinful, CHII 23.84-94; signified by
cultivation, CHII 26.101-10;
signified by walls, CHII 28.73-82;
the saved may not vaunt,
CHII 35.63-70; Christ chose simple
disciples, LS 5.219-26; in prayer,
Supp 5.180-84; in almsgiving,
Supp 30.55-68; in fasting,
Supp 30.69-74; monastic,
W 10a.45-48.

HYPOCRISY: general expositions,
CHI 35.532-34, **CHII 26**,
Supp 13.172-82, W 10c.8-18; in

repentance, B 2.25; of Judas, B 6.69;
signified by Herod, CHI 7.118-20;
false shepherds, CHI 17.240-42;
false works, CHI 27.398,
CHI 35.534-36; hypocrites signified
by hollow reeds, Supp 4.227-30;
signified by choking on a gnat,
Supp 13.162-71; of teachers during
last days, W 5.20-22; most hateful to
God, W 9.107-13; of Antichrist,
W 9.113-49.

I

IDLE SPEECH: *see* LANGUAGE.

IDOLATRY: *see also* APOSTASY,
THE DEVIL, DEVILS, ERROR, THE
HEATHEN, HERESY; general
expositions, LS 17.47-51,
Supp 18.281-86, **Supp 21, W 12**;
pagan temples will fall on the day of
judgement, B 7.93, V 15.113-17
(Vs 15.89-92); Simon Magus claims
to be the son of God, B 15.175;
St Martin's campaign against,
B 18.221-23, CHII 34.154-96,
LS 31.388-483, 706-21, 1229-55,
V 18.154-207 (Vs 18.92-132);
saints destroy idols and temples,
B 18.221-23, CHI 29.420,
LS 2.369-79, 383-88, LS 4.160-69,
362-79, LS 14.134-50,
LS 22.154-58, LS 31.388-483,
1229-55, V 18.154-207
(Vs 18.92-132); St Andrew's
campaign against, **B 19**,
CHI 38.586-88; its origins,
CHI 1.22-24, CHI 26.366,

Supp 21.115-17, W 12.50; Mars,
Supp 21.126-32, 170-71,
W 12.58-65; a ploy of the devil's,
Supp 21.159-65; apostles'
campaigns against, Supp 21.511-20;
Serapis, Supp 21.521-71; child
sacrifice, Supp 21.565-71; Egyptian
idols fall over at the approach of the
child Christ, V 6.69-80
(Vf 6.78-90); Rogationtide a
reclaimed pagan feast-day, V 11.1-8
(Vs 11.1-8), V 12.1-11 (Vs 12.1-9);
the devil compels men to,
W 6.82-95.

IDOLS: *see* IDOLATRY.

THE IMMACULATE
CONCEPTION: *see also* THE
ANNUNCIATION, THE HOLY SPIRIT,
THE INCARNATION, THE NATIVITY,
[appendix 1: MARY, THE MOTHER OF
CHRIST]; narrations and general
expositions, CHI 31.460,
V 5.125-38 (Vf 5.142-55); the Holy
Spirit's part in, V 10.16-18
(Vs 10.13-15).

THE INCARNATION: *see also*
CHRIST, THE IMMACULATE
CONCEPTION, THE NATIVITY, THE
TRINITY; general expositions, **B9**,
CHI 12.182, CHI 19.260,
CHI 24.338-40, CHI 31.458-60,
CHI 39.600, CHI 40.610,
CHII 1.1-17, 32-46, 70-73,
CHII 4.45-51, Supp 1.403-409,
Supp 6.262-65, Supp 8.219-27,
Supp 10.74-79, 147-58,

Supp 11.6-11, Supp 11a.226-30,
V 8.52-54 (Vf 8.57-60), V 10.9-25
(Vs 10.8-19), V 16.127-38
(Vs 16.99-108), W 6.134-53; Mary
conceived at the Annunciation,
B 1.3; Christ humbled himself to
become human, B 1.5, 11-13,
B 2.23, B 6.65-67, B 8.103,
B 9.105, CHI 2.32, 36, CHI 9.138,
140, CHI 21.300, CHI 22.320,
CHI 29.426, CHI 40.610,
CHII 31.60-66, V 5.1-6 (Vf 5.1-7);
Mary's womb Christ's bridal bower,
B 1.9-11; Mary's womb Solomon's
bed, B 1.11; Christ went to earth
without moving, B 2.19; had other
creatures needed salvation Christ
would have come in their forms,
B 3.29; Christ returned to heaven in
human form, B 11.123; recounted by
Christ, B 13.155; unites angels with
men, CHI 2.32, 38; conferred human
nature on Christ, CHI 2.42; indicated
by the phrase 'Son of Man',
CHI 3.48, CHI 40.610; fulfils God's
revelations to Moses,
CHII 22.50-58; made humankind
into the children of God,
CHII 35.74-81; as exile,
CHII 38.38-44.

INCENSE: signifies worship,
CHI 7.116; signifies prayer,
CHI 7.116-18, CHII 40.181-87.

INCEST: *see also* FORNICATION,
SEXUALITY; of Jupiter, LS 5.172-77,
LS 8.66-81, Supp 21.108-17,

W 12.44-50; of Venus, LS 8.66-81, Supp 21.115-17; allowed in the early age of the world, LS 10.215-17; of Minerva, Supp 21.115-17.

INNOCENCE: the devil forfeited his claim to the damned by causing the death of an innocent man, B 7.85-87, CHI 1.26, CHI 14.216, CHI 20.292; of Adam and Eve, CHI 1.18; signified by a lamb, CHI 9.140; signified by pigeons, CHI 9.142; signified by a dove, CHI 22.320, CHI 30.444, V 17.77-82 (Vs 17.61-65); of Christ, CHI 22.320; and wisdom, CHI 22.320-22; of children, CHI 34.512-14; sometimes confused with slackness, CHII 3.179.

INSECTS: *see also* ANIMALS, BEES; flea and louse infestation a consequence of the fall, Supp 21.45-48.

INTELLECT: *see also* KNOWLEDGE, MEMORY, REASON; part of the soul's resemblance to the Trinity, CHI 20.288-90, LS 1.112-22, LS 34.168-70; understanding a gift of the spirit, CHI 22.322, CHII 25.64-71, Supp 9.139-49, W 9.34-35; inner and outer understanding, CHII 38.49-52, 137-38; thought equated with the soul, V 22.152-56 (Vs 22.121-24); stupidity condemned, W 11.162-68.

INTERCESSION: *see also* APOSTLES, FORGIVENESS, HEALING, PRAYER, REPENTANCE, SAINTS; prayers for the dead, B 10.113, CHII 21.77-79, 130-61, LS 25.471-80, Supp 11.229-42; of the saints, CHI 11.174, CHI 36.546, CHI 37.556, LS 21.284-89, V 12.37-42 (Vs 12.30-34); examples of its efficacy, CHI 35.534-36, LS 3.169-200; of St Clement, CHI 37.564-66; of the apostles, CHII 8.58-65; of priests, CHII 19.116-20; intercessory prayer, CHII 30.199-203, CHII 35.123-27, Supp 17.99-112; none for the damned, CHII 39.192-98, Supp 11.220-24, 242, 268-72; of Abraham, LS 13.190-220; of monks, LS 13.216-20, Supp 11.164-76; of Christ, Supp 8.205-12; almsgiving a mode of, Supp 11.208-12; of souls in heaven, Supp 11.236-39; none after death, V 14.45-53 (Vs 14.37-43), Mary, St Peter, and St Michael each intercede for one third of the damned on the day of judgement, V 15.142-71 (Vs 15.111-34).

ISRAEL: *see* THE JEWS [appendix 2: JERUSALEM].

J

THE JEWS: *see also* THE ARK OF THE COVENANT, CIRCUMCISION, THE LAW OF MOSES, PASSOVER, THE PENTATEUCH, PHARISEES, THE SABBATH, SCRIPTURE [appendix 2:

Christians question St Peter's mission to the gentiles, LS 10.171-94; their guilt, LS 11.317-23; the Exodus, LS 13.1-5; England's contemporary situation like Israel's LS 13.175-81; the Maccabean revolt, Jewish martyrs, **LS 25**; forced conversions to paganism under Antiochus Ephiphanes, LS 25.15-24; dietary laws, LS 25.35-103; their concealment of the true cross, LS 27.4-5; the recalcitrance of the Israelites, Supp 20.38-39, 68-112, 165-202, 304-32, 357-60, W 19.41-85.

JUDGES: *see also* BISHOPS, KINGS, LAW, THE LAW OF MOSES; false judges, B 5.61-63, CHII 19.141-52, LS 19.233-38, W 11.175-80; duties of, B 5.63, CHII 19.127-41, LS 19.239-47, W 10c.164-68; Christ as judge, B 14.163, CHI 3.48, CHI 21.308-10; and mercy, CHII 19.132-39, Supp 13.88-105.

K

KINGS: *see also* BISHOPS, JUDGES, LAW; general expositions, **Supp 9**; the people's shepherd, B 4.45; Augustus' rule signifies Christ's peace, CHI 2.32; Christ recognized as king by the magi, CHI 7.106-108; gold signifies royalty, CHI 7.116-18; must be chosen by nation, CHI 14.212; must not be overthrown, CHI 14.212; Christ did

not make his apostles kings, CHI 16.232; wolf signifies tyrants, CHI 17.242; the righteous rule their bodies like kings, CHI 24.346; Christ chose fishermen before emperors, CHI 38.578; God rules like a king in a hall, CHII 5.39-41; Constantine the model of, CHII 18.1-7; duties of, CHII 19.91-99, Supp 9.46-63; soul sits in the throne of the body like, LS 1.195-96; should be righteous, LS 13.124; of Israel, **LS 18**; earthly and heavenly, LS 30.120-25; king and *witan*, Supp 9.46-54; Christ's substitute on earth, Supp 9.46-63; delegation of military affairs to generals, **Supp 22**; rise and fall of kings during the last days, V 15.31-58 (Vs 15.26-47); good government, W 10c.164-68.

KNEELING: men should not kneel on Sundays, LS 12.3-7.

KNOWLEDGE: *see also* INTELLECT, MEMORY, WISDOM; a gift of the spirit, CHI 22.322, CHII 25.64-71, Supp 9.139-49, W 9.34-35.

L

LABOUR: *see also* ACTIVE LIFE, THE FALL OF ADAM AND EVE, GOOD WORKS; every man's works will be tested by fire on the day of judgement, CHII 40.232-38; patriarchs and prophets fortified by,

V 7.22-24 (Vf 7.24-26); of the apostles, V 7.27-31 (Vf 7.29-33); difficulty of a holy life, V 7.31-34 (Vf 7.33-36); necessary for the soul, V 7.60-71 (Vf 7.65-78); spiritual, V 14.86-98 (Vs 14.69-78); for monks, W 10a.38-48).

LAMB: *see also* ANIMALS, PASSOVER, SHEEP; signifies innocence, CHI 9.140; signifies Christ, CHI 22.312, CHI 25.358, CHI 38.590, CHII 3.85-90, CHII 15.38-63, 225-64; at Passover, CHI 22.312, CHI 3.79-90; St Paul converted from wolf to lamb, CHI 27.390; signifies teachers, CHII 36.57-62.

LAMENESS: *see also* DISEASE; signifies those who do not fulfil God's commandments, Supp 2.78-79.

LAMP: *see* also LIGHT; lamp oil signifies love, CHII 39.47-54; lamps signify good works, CHII 39.54-64; trimmed lamps signify preparedness for the day of judgement, CHII 39.136-38; teachers signified by lanterns, V 11.9-20 (Vs 11.9-17).

LANGUAGE: *see also* SILENCE, THE TOWER OF BABEL; translation, CHI pref.2, CHI 30.436, LS 15.108-10; perception of its beauty is not enough, CHI 12.186; Latin a humble tongue beside Hebrew, CHII 5.273-87; Latin

conceals Christ's words, CHII 22.186-191; at the Pentecost, CHII 32.95-105, Supp 7.195-202, Supp 11.54-71; speech signified by silver, CHII 40.238-43; of the gospels, LS 15.127-73; idle speech pleases the devil, V 20.5-15 (Vs 20.4-12).

LAST DAYS: *see also* ANTICHRIST, THE DAY OF JUDGEMENT; general narrations and expositions, **B 10, CHI pref, V 15 (Vs 15), W 2, W 3, W 4, W 5, W 20BH, W 20C, W 20EI**; the world has entered, B 5.59, B 10.107-109, B 11.117-19, CHI pref.2-4, CHI 21.298, CHI 38.578-80, CHI 40.610, CHII 22.191-202; the seven days leading up to the day of judgement, B 7.91-95, V 15.79-140 (Vs 15.63-110); love grows cold during, B 10.109, B 15.171, Supp 18.326-37, W 5.26-32; the need of learning during, **CHI pref**, CHII 22.191-202; the coming of false Christs, **CHI pref**, W 2.37-42; Enoch and Elijah will return during, CHI 21.306-308, CHI 25.356; spread of warfare during, CHII 37.29-33, W 2.43-49; false prophets and teachers during, LS 31.842-44, Supp 18.383-96, W 2.54-55, W 5.20-22; miracles cease during, LS 35.346-60, Supp 18.356-65, W 3.48-49, W 5.58-64; Viking invasions associated with, W 3.20-26; God conceals his power during,

W 3.45-58; God will cut short,
W 4.11-14; W 5.108-13; pride
during, W 5.19; collapse of family
loyalties during, W 5.98-100,
W 20BH.56-58, 77-81,
W 20C.69-71, 84-92,
W 20EI.61-63, 92-95.

THE LAST SUPPER: *see also* THE
PASSION; narrated, CHII 14.23-78.

LAW: *see also* JUDGES, KINGS, THE
LAW OF MOSES, OATHS; one law of
love for all humankind,
LS 11.348-52; should guide the
nation, LS 13.126-27; and the spirit,
LS 17.15-29; capital punishment,
LS 19.178-80; necessity of,
Supp 13.86-96; the devil claims a
legal right to the damned,
V 10.63-100 (Vs 10.48-76);
punishment of monastic
misdemeanours, W 10a.50-57; legal
rights abused, W 20BH.33-37,
42-43, W 20C.39-44, 48-53,
W 20EI.37-42, 47-48; runaway
slaves murder without paying
wergild, W 20C.97-103,
W 20EI.100-106; cowardly laws in
England, W 20C.103-105,
W 20EI.106-109; those who disobey
divine law should be punished by
secular law, W 21.9-14, 26-31.

THE LAW OF MOSES: *see also*
THE JEWS, LAW, THE PENTATEUCH,
SCRIPTURE; framed and handed down
by God, CHI 1.24, CHI 22.312,
CHII 12.120-177, Supp 20.27-37,

W 10c.20-31; ordains death for
adultery, CHI 2.40-42, CHI 13.196;
signified by Christ's circumcision,
CHI 6.94; and disease, CHI 8.122,
124-26; Christ the lord of,
CHI 8.122; and purification,
CHI 9.134, 138-40; spiritual
meanings of, CHI 9.142,
CHI 12.186, CHI 27.390,
CHII 8.110-19, CHII 12.165-77,
CHII 15.34-85; signified by bread,
CHI 12.186, 188, CHII 25.19-34;
was written about Christ,
CHI 12.186; law-abiding Jews
signified by a tame ass, CHI 14.208;
foreshadows the New Testament,
CHI 25.354-56; easier than the law
of Christ, CHI 25.358,
Supp 15.25-38, 105-24; St Paul's
zeal for, CHI 27.388; allowed the
annihilation of enemies, CHI 35.522,
CHII 12.439-45; inferior to the
beatitudes, CHI 36.548; its
exhaustion, CHII 4.58-67; Christ's
transformation of, CHII 4.92-99,
CHII 12.458-64; the decalogue,
CHII 12.221-333; made the Jews
proud, CHII 28.17-25; the Holy
Spirit inscribed the tables of,
Supp 4.145-49; allowed hatred of
enemies, Supp 15.80-89; clarified by
Christ, W 10c.31-34.

LEFT: *see also* RIGHT; the left side
of St Peter's boat signifies the men
of this world, CHII 16.153-63;
signifies evil, Supp 14.167-75; left
hand signifies worldly pride,
Supp 30.61-68.

LENT: *see also*; FASTING, REPENTANCE; general expositions, B 3.35-39, **CHII 7,** Supp 11a.128-32, **W 14**; fasts during, B 3.35, LS 12.11-15, 75-78, W 14.15-18, 25-31; calculation of its length, B 3.35; its duration (1/10 year) signifies tithing, B 3.35, CHI 11.178; signifies this world, B 3.35; purifies, B 3.37-39.

LEPROSY: *see also* DISEASE; signifies humankind, CHI 8.122; in the law of Moses, CHI 8.122; Christ appears as a leper, CHI 23.336-38; St Martin cures with a kiss, CHII 34.211-13.

LEVITATION: of ascetic saints, LS 23b.260-87.

LIES: *see* DECEIT.

LIFE: *see also* ANGELS, ANIMALS, DEATH, MAN, THE EARTH, THE WORLD; transience of, B 5.59, B 6.73, V 17.112-18 (Vs 17.88-92); three kinds of, LS 1.25-33, V 9.37-40 (Vs 9.31-33); life in England feebler than elsewhere because of its climate, LS 13.106-109; men feebler now than in former times, LS 13.110; present life to be transformed on the day of judgement, V 4.8-16 (Vf 4.9-18); a theatre of choice, V 4.89-96 (Vf 4.99-106); God's desire that we should earn eternal life, W 13.14-19.

LIGHT: *see also* DARKNESS, LAMP, NIGHT; signifies Christ, B 2.17, B 9.105-107, CHI 2.36, CHI 9.144, CHI 35.530, LS 28.108-12, LS 29.14-16, Supp 1.286-98, 321-35, Supp 6.343-48, LS 28.108-12, LS 29.14-16, V 17.121-23 (Vs 17.93-95); in processions, CHI 9.150; we must pray for, CHI 10.158-60; weapon of the faithful, CHI 39.604; God's light confers broader vision, CHII 11.536-46; preached by John the Baptist, Supp 1.299-316; signifies the apostles, Supp 1.317-20.

LIGHTNING: sent to help Christians in war, B 17.203, CHI 34.504-506; terror of, CHI 15.222-24; on Mt Sinai, CHII 12.232-34; destroys heathen temples, CHII 33.253-59; heralds God, LS 36.226-31.

LILY: *see also* FLOWERS; symbol of purity, CHI 30.444, LS 34.72-77; signifies Christ's body, LS 34.112-13.

LION: *see also* ANIMALS; signifies Christ, CHI 25.358; Daniel in the lion's den, CHI 37.570-72, Supp 21.300-49, 451-93; Judas Maccabeus likened to, LS 25.282-83; St Guthlac attacked by devil in lion's form, V 23.13-20 (Vs 23.9-14).

M

MADNESS: *see also* DEVILS, EXORCISM, HEALING; signifies the state of the heathen soul, CHII 8.30-34; the result of demonic possession, CHII 13.100-101; in animals, CHII 34.259-61.

THE MAGI: *see also* ASTROLOGY, THE HOLY INNOCENTS, THE NATIVITY [appendix 1: HEROD]; their knowledge of God's purpose, CHI 7.104-106; signify the gentiles, CHI 7.106; acknowledge Christ's divine and human natures, CHI 7.106-108; signify humankind's return to paradise, CHI 7.118.

MAGIC: *see* SORCERY.

THE MAGNIFICAT: *see also* THE CREED, THE LORD's PRAYER, PRAYER [appendix 1: MARY THE MOTHER OF CHRIST]; explicated, B 13.157-59, CHI 13.202-204.

MAN: *see also* THE BODY, CHRISTIANS, DEATH, THE FALL OF ADAM AND EVE, LIFE, OLD AGE, SOCIETY, THE SOUL, WOMAN, THE WORLD; the griefs of human existence, B 5.59-61, CHI 32.488-90, CHII 13.126-29; created for eternal life, B 5.61; life fleeting, B 5.59, B 6.73, V 17.112-18 (Vs 17.88-92); created to replace fallen angels, B 11.121,

CHI 1.12, CHI 2.32, CHI 13.192, CHI 14.214, CHI 15.222, CHI 24.342-44, CHII 5.183-94, W 6.34-39; men called 'gods', CHI 2.40, Supp 1.357-85, Supp 21.669-73; not ruled by the stars, CHI 7.110; present existence like a prison, CHI 10.154; signified by an ass, CHI 14.208; the soul distinguishes men from animals, CHI 20.276, CHI 21.302; resembles to the Trinity, CHI 20.288-90, LS 1.112-22, LS 34.166-70; shares something with all creation, CHI 21.302; created to be Christ's brother, CHII 1.29-31; human life paralleled by the ages of the world, CHII 5.88-106; men are the house of God, CHII 40.118-25; men must uphold one another like stones in a wall, CHII 40.125-29; possesses a natural love of the good, LS 1.88-89; God's steward, Supp 16.49-54; lost natural instinct for the good in the fall, Supp 21.52-55; creaturely obligation toward Creator, V 22.129-56 (Vs 22.103-24).

MANNA: general expositions, Supp 20.10-21; discovered in the tomb of St John the Evangelist, CHI 4.76; signifies the eucharist, CHII 12.206-14, CHII 15.174-208; tasted like one's favourite food, Supp 20.18-21, 122-27; signifies Christ, Supp 20.128-31.

MARRIAGE: *see also* ADULTERY, CELIBACY, CHASTITY, DIVORCE,

FORNICATION, PARENTHOOD, SEXUALITY, VIRGINITY, THE WEDDING AT CANA, WOMAN; Mary's womb Christ's bridal bower, B 1.9-11; the wedding at Cana, CHI 4.58, **CHII 4**; married apostles left their wives to follow Christ, CHI 4.58, CHII 6.158-66, LS 10. 202-10, LS 16.184-88; its excellence, CHI 9.148, CHII 4.294-305, CHII 6.115-26; inferior to virginity, CHI 9.148, CHII 4.294-305, CHII 6.115-35, Supp 19.73-89; St Paul's admonition to husbands and wives, CHI 26.378; of Herod, CHI 32.478; the Church is Christ's bride, CHI 35.520, CHII 1.91-109, CHII 4.29-36; only for the begetting of children, CHII 6.127-31, Supp 19.112-18; conjugal responsibilities, CHII 19.153-69, Supp 19.90-104; a symbol of lust, CHII 23.71-76, its rejection by saints, LS 7.14-62, 370-80, LS 9.35-67, LS 10.249-68, LS 33.31-155, LS 36.271-402; of Jewish priests, LS 10.218-21.

MARTYRDOM: *see also* CONVERSION, SAINTS, TORTURE; general expositions, CHI 36.542-44, LS 16.191-202, Supp 9.167-71, Supp 18.345-55; of St Peter, **B 15**, CHI 26.382-84, LS 10.1-15; of St Paul, **B 15**, CHI 26.382-84; God permits for purification, CHI pref.6; of St Stephen, **CHI 3**, CHII 2.186-89; the mothers of the Holy Innocents are also martyrs,

CHI 5.84; of Mary, CHI 9.146, CHI 30.444; martyrs signified by crowds on Palm Sunday, CHI 14.212; kinds of, CHI 14.212, CHII 37.132-54; signified by roses, CHI 30.444, LS 34.72-77, 100-109; abstaining from sin constitutes a kind of martyrdom, CHI 36.544; God saves martyrs, CHI 37.574; of St Andrew, CHI 38.590-98; of St Eventius and St Theodolus, CHII 18.67-156; martyrs confessors of Christ, CHII 38.192-212; of St Eugenia, LS 2.389-413; Christ allowed Christians to flee martyrdom, LS 5.327-34; of St Agnes, LS 7.216-45; of St Agatha, LS 8.97-206; constitutes baptism in one's own blood, LS 11.293-98; persecutors only serve God's purpose, LS 11.324-30; of St George, LS 14.41-170; of St Alban, LS 19.80-122; of St Apollinaris, LS 22.159-250; of St Abdon, LS 24.40-67; Jewish martyrs, **LS 25**; of St Maurice and his companions, LS 28.54-116; of St Denis, LS 29.226-300; of St Eustace, LS 30.391-472; of St Edmund, LS 32.101-26; of St Cecilia, LS 34.287-361; the glory of, LS 34.293-99; Ælfric's doubts about the narrative of St Thomas', LS 36.1-12; of St Thomas, LS 36.407-24; renewed during the last days, V 15.31-38 (Vs 15.26-31).

MASS: *see* CHURCHES, THE EUCHARIST, PRIESTS.

MEDICINE: *see* DISEASE, HEALING.

MEMORY: *see also* INTELLECT, REASON, THE SOUL; part of man's resemblance to the Trinity, CHI 20.288-90, LS 1.112-22, LS 34.168-70.

MERCHANTS: *see also* WEALTH; in the temple of Solomon, CHI 28.406, 410-12; sellers of doves signify those who teach merely for profit, CHI 28.412; proper conduct of, CHII 19.235-38; churches not to be sold, CHII 40.293-98, LS 19.248-54; power to heal not to be sold, LS 5.182-205; eternal life to be purchased with good works, LS 12.100-40; compel the servant of the seven sleepers of Ephesus to reveal their cave, LS 23.560-627; spiritual merchants, V 11.63-70 (Vs 11.52-57).

MERCY: *see also* FORGIVENESS, REPENTANCE; God's for Adam and Eve, CHI 1.18-20, CHI 13.192, CHII 1.18-27, V 1E.1-7, V 5.6-9 (Vf 5.7-10), W 7.38-49; God's for humankind, CHI 4.68, CHI 7.112, CHI 14.210, CHII 5.210-33, CHII 19.47-54, Supp 13.72-85, V 1E.1-7, W 6.154-58; in the beatitudes, CHI 36.552; medicine for sin, CHII 7.46-51; in judges, CHII 19.132-39, Supp 13.97-105; Christian duty of, CHII 33.49-54, 227-34, Supp 13.37-47, 67-90; lack

of signified by withered hand, Supp 2.82-90; cure for covetousness, V 20.96-97 (Vs 20.75-76).

MILK: signifies teaching, Supp 19.1-9.

MIND: *see* INTELLECT, MEMORY, REASON, THE SOUL.

MIRACLES: *see also* CONVERSION, DEVILS, HEALING, LEVITATION, TORTURE; the apostles' were genuine, B 15.173; Antichrist's false miracles, CHI pref.4-6, CHII 30.93-97, Supp 18.287-306; Christ performed miracles to strengthen the apostles' faith, CHI 10.152-54; God performs daily, CHI 12.184; no longer necessary for faith, CHI 21.304; bodily versus spiritual, CHI 21.306; disease an occasion for, CHI 31.474; will cease during the last days, LS 35.346-60, Supp 18.356-65, W 3.48-49, W 5.58-64; at Christ's birth, V 5.57-66 (Vf 5.66-77), V 6 (Vf 6).

MONASTERIES: *see* MONKS.

MONKS: *see also* ACTIVE LIFE, BISHOPS, CONTEMPLATIVE LIFE, PRIESTS; duties of, B 4.47-49, CHII 20.187-98, **W 10a**; false monks, CHI 27.398, CHI 35.534-36, LS 31.341-65, 792-830; those who vacillate in monastic life signified by Ananias and Sapphira, CHI 27.398;

Judas the companion of those who defraud monasteries of property, CHI 27.398; solitary, CHI 36.544; poverty of, CHI 36.550; St Gregory founds monasteries at his own expense, CHII 9.32-36; St Benedict's career, **CHII 11**; St Benedict's monks tempted by female dancers, CHII 11.153-70; must be ordained by a teacher, CHII 40.301-304; lay founders of monasteries must not interfere with them, CHII 40.304-11; St Eugenia disguised as, LS 2.88-97; St Basil's rule stricter than St Benedict's, LS 3.145-52; England's woes the result of contempt for monastic life, LS 13.147-55; must not engage in worldly warfare, LS 25.823-62; St Martin's early calling to monastic life, LS 31.26-30; the conduct of St Martin's monastery, LS 31.320-40; monasteries' share of tithes, Supp 30.86-105; decline in monastic vocations, V 11.90-99 (Vs 11.73-79); prone to sloth, V 20.106-108 (Vs 20.83-85); the office of the hours, W 10a.28-33; truancy, W 10a.36-38; teaching in monasteries, W 10a.43-45; silence in monasteries, W 10a.48-50; punishment of monastic misdemeanours, W 10a.50-56; monastic orders held in contempt, W 20BH.33-37, W 20C.39-44, W 20EI.37-42.

MONEY: *see* ALMSGIVING, COINS, GOLD, MERCHANTS, POVERTY, WEALTH.

MOON: *see also* STARS, SUN, THE HEAVENS; signifies the world, B 2.17, CHI 10.154, CHII 12.425-38; living things stronger during the full moon, CHI 6.102; and the tides, CHI 6.102; worship of, CHI 26.366, Supp 21.82-84, W 12.17-21; Mary compared with, CHI 30.444; eclipses of, CHI 40.608-10; during the last days, CHI 40.608-10; transformation of after the day of judgement, CHI 40.616-18, Supp 11.513-16, Supp 21.62-65; obeys the Creator, CHII 33.235-39; on the day of judgement, Supp 11.287-89, V 2.6-7 (Vf 2.7-8), V 15.57-58 (Vs 15.47), V 21.164-65 (Vs 21.126-27); lost its brightness after the fall of Adam and Eve, Supp 21.56-61; Monday named for, Supp 21.166-70; transfigured body of the blessed likened to, V 4.160-61 (Vf 4.178-80); grows dark to punish sin, W 3.42-43; its darkening signifies Christians' inability to perform miracles during the reign of Antichrist, W 3.48-49.

MORNING: *see also* DAY, MORNING STAR; signifies the world to come, CHII 3.174-76; signifies teaching, LS 5.105-11.

MORNING STAR: *see also* DAY, MORNING, STARS; signifies John the

Baptist, B 14.163, CHI 25.354.

MOTHER: *see* PARENTHOOD.
MOUNTAINS: *see also* VALLEY;
signify heaven, CHI 8.120,
CHII 24.92-99, 131-39,
LS 36.77-83; signify God's
commandments, CHI 36.548; prayer
upon, Supp 5.159-79; symbol of
exaltation, Supp 5.178-79; men flee
to on the day of judgement,
V 15.118-28 (V 15.93-101).

MURDER: *see also*
ASSASSINATION, POISON, the wealthy
who refuse to give alms guilty of,
B 4.53, CHII 12.320-25; three kinds
of, B 5.63-65; of Abel,
CHII 4.104-10, LS 16.13-15,
W 6.53-56; in the decalogue,
CHII 12.320-25; physical and
spiritual, LS 13.305-308; and wrath,
Supp 15.125-42; the greatest sin
after blasphemy, Supp 24.12-14;
runaway slaves kill without paying
wergild, W 20c.97-103,
W 20EI.100-106.

MUSIC: *see also* POETRY,
TRUMPET; heavenly music eases the
soul's departure from the body,
Supp 27.60-82; the devil's harping,
V 10.83-87 (Vs 10.63-66); Isaiah's
denunciation of 'gleemen',
W 11.144-45.

MYRRH: signifies death,
CHI 7.116; signifies continence,
CHI 7.118.

MYSTERY: Christ's words
mysterious, B 2.17; of miracles,
CHI 10.154.

N

THE NATIVITY: *see also* THE
ANNUNCIATION, CHRIST, THE
IMMACULATE CONCEPTION, THE
INCARNATION [appendix 1: MARY, THE
MOTHER OF CHRIST]; narrations and
general expositions, **B 9, CHI 2,
CHII 1, LS 1,** Supp 11a.69-85, **V 5
(Vf 5), V 6 (Vf 6),** V 10.9-25
(Vs 10.8-19), W 7.38-49; and
Christ's resurrection, CHI 15.222;
and St John the Baptist's,
CHI 25.356; angels and good will,
CHI 38.582-84; miracles at Christ's
birth, V 5.57-66 (Vf 5.66-77), **V 6
(Vf 6);** the animals present signify
Christians, V 5.139-50
(Vf 5.156-68); the birth of Antichrist
contrasted with, W 5.37-40.

NEW YEAR: the history of its
observance, CHI 6.98-100.

NIGHT: *see also* DARKNESS, DAY,
LIGHT; signifies this world,
CHI 18.248, CHII 39.104-12;
signifies pagan ignorance of Christ,
CHI 39.602-604; signifies the devil,
CHI 39.604; the end of signifies the
day of judgement, CHII 24.139-44;
signifies ignorance, Supp 12.69-77;
signifies persecution by Antichrist,
Supp 18.86-89.

NORTH: *see also* EAST, WEST; Lucifer seeks a realm in the north of heaven, CHI 1.10.

NUMEROLOGY: one thousand a perfect number, CHI 12.188; one hundred a perfect number, CHI 24.338, CHI 27.396; numerological exegesis, Supp 2.139-50.

NUNS: *see* ACTIVE LIFE, THE CHURCH, CONTEMPLATIVE LIFE, MONKS, WOMAN.

O

OATHS: *see also* BAPTISM, CURSING, OATHS; God forbids, CHI 32.482, Supp 24.1-3; Isaac's oath taken on Abraham's thigh, CHII 13.190-204; oathbreaking, W 20BH.81-85, W 20C.92-96, W 20EI.95-99.

OBEDIENCE: *see also* THE FAITHFUL, FREE WILL; general expositions, CHII 13.81-94, Supp 30.16-28, W 10c.8-18; what God desires most in tithing, B 4.39; the disobedient like the heathen, B 4.49; condition of Adam's bliss, CHI 1.14-16; of women, CHI 6.98; humility incomplete without, CHII 3.98-107; of John the Baptist, CHII 3.101-107, V 16.48-56 (Vs 16.36-42); a test of love, CHII 19.22-32, Supp 10.29-35; of the young, LS 13.118; England's and

Israel's blessedness dependent upon, LS 13.156-74; disobedience signified by blindness, deafness and lameness, Supp 2.76-81; of Mary, Supp 4.287-94; God tolerates the disobedient, Supp 13.48-53; murmuring forbidden, Supp 20.390-400; a remedy for fornication, V 20.86-88 (Vs 20.68-69); humankind's daily disobedience, V 22.193-203 (Vs 22.153-60), W 3.14-18; love of God founded upon, W 8c.23-26; to bishops, W 17.28-41, 50-56.

OIL: *see also* OLIVE; wells flowed with on the night of the Nativity, V 6.25-29 (Vf 6.29-33).

OLD AGE: *see also* THE BODY, DEATH, DISEASE; signified by the west, CHI 8.130; ills of itemized, CHI 32.490, V 9.89-97 (Vs 9.70-76); of the world, CHI 40.614; and sexuality, CHII 19.170-78; the aged should be pious, LS 13.117; a foretaste of hell, V 9.89-97 (Vs 9.70-76).

OLIVE: its uses, Supp 16.132-41.

ORIGINAL SIN: *see* THE FALL OF ADAM AND EVE, SIN.

OX: *see also* ANIMALS; sellers of oxen signify false teachers, CHI 28.412; signify the five senses, CHII 23.43-62.

P

PARABLES: *see also* SCRIPTURE, TEACHING; nature of, Supp 8.167-78, Supp 13.126-27.

PARADISE: *see* THE CREATION, THE FALL OF ADAM AND EVE, HEAVEN.

PARENTHOOD: *see also* CHILDREN; proper conduct in, B 10.109, CHII 19.186-214, Supp 19.54-60; the mothers of the Holy Innocents are also martyrs, CHI 5.84; children not responsible for parents' sins, CHI 7.114; St Paul's admonitions to parents, CHI 26.378; the Church is the mother of Christians, CHI 33.494, CHI 35.520, CHII 1.91-109, CHII 4.29-36, CHII 12.312-17, CHII 39.87-92, Supp 6.192-95, Supp 12.130, W 10c.41-54; children cursed by their mother, CHII 2.98-176; honouring parents, CHII 12.312-17; God's love like a mother's, LS 23.251-53; collapse of family loyalties during the last days, W 5.98-100, W 20BH.56-58, 77-81, W 20C.69-71, 84-92, W 20EI.61-63, 92-95.

THE PASSION: *see also* THE CROSS, THE HARROWING OF HELL, THE JEWS, THE LAST SUPPER, THE RESURRECTION; narrations and general expositions, B 1.7, **B 6**, B 8.97, CHI 1.26-28, CHI 14.216, **CHII 14**, Supp 11a.133-41, **V 1** (**Vf 1**), V 2.83-89 (Vf 2.111-17); V 8.54-68 (Vf 8.60-75), W 6.181-88, W 13.36-41; Christ foretells to strengthen his disciples, B 2.15-17, CHI 10.152; Christ's patience in, B 2.23; Christ's fearlessness in, B 6.67; Pilate's account of, B 15.177; acknowledged by heaven and earth, CHI 7.108, CHI 15.228, CHII 14.287-93, LS 29.9-16, V 1.235-39 (Vf 1.300-305), V 16.81-88 (Vs 16.61-67); signified by the Passover lamb, CHI 22.312, CHII 15.38-52; and Mary, CHI 30.444; Christ's mercy toward his executioner, CHII 2.181-83; and the birth of the Church, CHII 4.100-104; signified by Saul's persecution of David, CHII 4.200-204; signified by Old Testament animal sacrifices, CHII 12.344-56; commemoration of, CHII 13.1-10; signified by Moses' bronze serpent, CHII 13.237-92, Supp 20.304-52; crown of thorns signifies Adam's curse, CHII 14.213-18; signified by water, Supp 2.130-33; signified by the Sabbath, Supp 2.247-50; signified by the murder of vineyard owner's son, Supp 3.124-32; Christ appears on the day of judgement as he appeared during the passion, Supp 11.291-95, V 15.138-40 (Vs 15.109-10), V 21.166-68 (Vs 21.128-30), W 2.65-69.

PASSOVER: *see also* EASTER;
narrations and general expositions,
CHI 22.310-12, CHII 15.8-68,
174-208, 324-36, Supp 20.113-21;
its association with Pentecost,
CHI 22.310.

PATER NOSTER: *see* THE LORD'S
PRAYER.

PATIENCE: *see also* FORTITUDE,
HUMILITY; of Christ, B 3.33,
CHI 11.170, 174, CHI 15.226,
CHI 38.592, CHII 13.107-17,
V 4.4-8 (Vf 4.4-9), V 16.118-26
(Vs 16.91-98); of God, B 3.33,
CHI 19.268-70, CHI 40.610,
LS 23b.384-91, Supp 15.39-54;
requires effort, CHI 25.360; its
power, CHII 6.106-14; of Job,
CHII 19.252-59, LS 16.36-54,
LS 30.126-27; of teachers,
CHII 36.57-68; the supreme virtue,
CHII 37.122-31, LS 28.125-56;
three kinds of, CHII 37.155-59;
examples of, CHII 37.164-201; in
the face of the tribulations of the last
days, LS 13.290-93; repels devils,
LS 17.205-12; of martyrs,
LS 28.125-31; of St Eustace,
LS 30.125-391; of St Martin,
LS 31.44-50; signified by Christ's
command that the bedridden should
take up his bed, Supp 2.192-208; a
remedy for wrath, V 20.101-103
(Vs 20.79-81).

PATRIARCHS: *see also* THE JEWS,
PROPHECY [appendix 1: ABRAHAM,

ISAAC, JACOB, JOSEPH]; general
expositions, CHI 36.540; signified
by oxen, CHI 35.522; signified by
vineyard workers, CHII 5.50-72; in
hell, CHII 5.143-60; God's care for,
LS 11.177-84; signified by
messengers sent to vineyard,
Supp 3.115-23; sowers of seed,
Supp 5.247-64.

PEACE: *see also* FORGIVENESS,
WAR; Christ's, CHI 2.32,
CHI 16.230-32, CHII 40.74-85,
Supp 10.120-26; Christ's signified
by the *pax romana*, CHI 2.32,
V 5.76-86 (Vf 5.90-101); Christ
brought peace between angels and
men, CHI 2.36-38, V 5.159-83
(Vf 5.186-206); 'Jerusalem' means
'vision of peace', CHI 14.210,
V 17.47-63 (Vs 17.38-50); in the
beatitudes, CHI 36.552; St Martin
enjoins upon his brethren,
CHII 34.272-84, V 18.223-30
(Vs 18.146-51); signified by the
name 'Solomon', CHII 40.74-85;
and mutual forgiveness,
Supp 15.191-213, V 6.90-91
(Vf 6.101-102); men couldn't fight
on the day of Christ's nativity,
V 6.16-22 (Vf 6.19-25); and love,
V 14.111-20 (Vs 14.89-96); mutual,
V 17.47-63 (Vs 17.38-50),
W 13.53-62.

PENANCE: *see* CONFESSION,
FORGIVENESS, REPENTANCE.

PENITENCE: *see* CONFESSION,

FORGIVENESS, REPENTANCE.

THE PENTATEUCH: *see also* THE JEWS, THE LAW OF MOSES, SCRIPTURE; signified by the miracle of the loaves and fish, CHI 12.186-88, CHII 25.19-34; once a secret, CHII 25.24-25; signified by five porticoes, Supp 2.59-67.

PENTECOST: *see also* THE APOSTLES, THE HOLY SPIRIT, LANGUAGE, PASSOVER, THE RESURRECTION; narrations and general expositions, **B 12, CHI 22,** Supp 2.177-83, Supp 9.130-57, **Supp 10,** Supp 11.54-71, Supp 11a.171-87; its effect upon the apostles, B 11.119; and the giving of the Law of Moses, CHII 12.221-25; reverses the curse of Babel, CHII 32.95-105, Supp 7.95-202, Supp 11.54-71.

PERSECUTION: *see also* ANTICHRIST, MARTYRDOM, SAINTS, TORTURE; during the last days, CHI pref.6, CHII 37.79-112, W 2.52-57, W 3.53-60, W 5.53-81; Saul's persecution of Christians, CHI 27.384-86, 388-90; under Decius, CHI 29.416; under Julian the Apostate, CHI 30.448-50; persecutors of the faithful come to bad ends, CHI 35.524-26; not to be deliberately sought for, CHI 36.552-54; rejoicing in, CHI 36.552-54; under Aurelian,

CHII 18.67-156; of the early Christians, CHII 37.66-106; of the Jews under Antiochus Epiphanes, **LS 25;** signified by night, Supp 18.86-89.

PHARISEES: *see also* THE JEWS, THE LAW OF MOSES, THE TEMPLE OF SOLOMON; possessed virtue, CHII 28.73-82; were mistaken about Christ, CHII 32.44-48.

PHILOSOPHY: *see also* REASON, TEACHING, WISDOM; and Christian teaching, CHI 4.60-62, LS 3.26-31, LS 4.184-94, LS 35.80-118; St Eugenia devoted to by her father, LS 2.18-23; St Basil's study of, LS 3.1-15; Julian the Apostate's study of, LS 3.16-18; St Gregory's study of, LS 3.19-20; abandoned as useless by the saints, LS 3.26-31, LS 4.184-94, LS 35.16-23; philosophers in Egypt saw signs of the crucifixion, LS 29.9-13;

PIETY: *see* FAITH.

PIGEONS: *see also* BIRDS, DOVE; signify love, CHI 9.140, 142; their innocence, V 17.77-82 (Vs 17.61-65).

PIGS: *see* SWINE.

POETRY: *see also* MUSIC; David's harping, Supp 27.71-82; inadequate to describe heaven's joys, V 9.193 (Vs 9.117); the devil's harping,

CHII 35.119-23; can be performed anywhere, CHII 40.144-47; Moses' example of, LS 13.6-29; shatters the devil's weapons, LS 13.50-54; the devil seeks to disrupt, LS 13.55-59; as speech to God, LS 13.60-67; sincerity in, LS 13.87-88; food for the soul, LS 13.89-90; must accompany medicine, LS 17.213-21; under old and new dispensations, Supp 5.159-204; on mountains, Supp 5.159-79; humility in, Supp 5.180-84; Jewish prayers in the temple of Solomon, Supp 5.190-93; of the apostles, Supp 8.73-78; and fasting, V 3.122-25 (Vf 3.133-37); purity essential for, V 14.99-111 (Vs 14.79-89); for others, V 14.111-20 (Vs 14.89-96).

PRIDE: *see also* CLOTHING, THE FALL OF THE ANGELS, FLATTERY, HUMILITY; general expositions, CHII 12.531-41, 556-59, **CHII 28**, V 2.90-96 (Vf 2.118-25), V 20.61-69 (Vs 20.50-55); the devil's, B 13.159, CHI pref.6, CHI 1.10, 14, CHI 9.138; CHI 11.170-72, LS 16.309-11, V 21.140-49 (Vs 21.107-14); good works useless if done on account of, CHI 8.122-24, CHII 39.71-78; the chief sin, CHI 11.170, V 20.61-69 (Vs 20.50-55); caused multiplication of languages, CHI 22.318; the Holy Spirit flees, CHI 25.362; signified by hills, CHI 25.362; the origin of sin, CHI 36.550; damns the sinful, CHII 23.84-94; of the Jews,

CHII 28.17-25, CHII 32.60-67; the proud will be humbled, CHII 28.92-96, 160-63; of Nebuchadnezzar, CHII 28.96-133; of Balshazzar, CHII 28.134-59; the saved must not vaunt, CHII 35.63-70; signified by birds, LS 16.163; of Antiochus Epiphanes, LS 25.6-14; of scribes and pharisees, Supp 15.55-79; the evil of boasting, Supp 17.190-202; caused Adam's fall, V 2.93-95 (Vf 2.122-25); signified by a bow, V 4.308-21 (Vf 4.340-54); signified by a tree, V 10.208-12 (Vs 10.156-59); signified by a tower, V 10.212-18 (Vs 10.159-62); signified by cliffs, V 10.212-18 (Vs 10.159-62); remedied by humility, V 20.68-69 (Vs 20.55); consequences of, V 20.66-67 (Vs 20.54-55); during the last days, W 5.20; Isaiah's denunciation of, W 11.125-32; presumptuous lack of trust in God, W 11.181-87.

PRIESTHOOD: *see* PRIESTS.

PRIESTS: *see also* BISHOPS, THE CHURCH, MONKS; duties of, B 4.43, CHII 19.104-111, CHII 20.186-87, W 1b.28-30; slack priests in hell, B 4.43; slack priests like rebel angels, B 4.49; wield St Peter's powers, CHI 26.370; of the early Church, CHI 36.544; Christ as priest, CHII 4.268-76; their efficacy affected by sin, CHII 19.116-20; shortage of effective priests,

CHII 36.33-40; Jewish,
LS 10.218-31; celibacy,
LS 10.222-31; their efficacy not
affected by sin, Supp 12.91-94,
W 8c.36-41; should not abandon
churches, Supp 14.195-206;
signified by ploughmen,
Supp 18.153-68; children dedicated
to God's service by their parents
ought not to demur, Supp 19.53-60;
respect for, Supp 20.274-303; Daniel
exposes false priests of Bel,
Supp 21.350-431; and the eucharist,
V 14.77-85 (Vs 14.62-68); false
priests during the last days,
V 15.10-28 (Vs 15.9-22).

PROCESSIONS: *see* RELICS,
ROGATIONTIDE.

PROPHECY: *see also* DIVINATION,
FATE, PATRIARCHS, SCRIPTURE,
SORCERY; Old Testament prophecies
of Christ, B 6.71, CHI 9.136,
CHI 12.190, CHI 13.192-194,
CHI 25.358, CHI 33.494,
CHI 36.540, CHI 39.600,
CHII 1.121-213, CHII 8.112-19,
CHII 23.30-37, LS 16.83-93,
Supp 9.163-65, V 1E.7-27,
V 10.9-25 (Vs 10.8-19); fulfilled by
the harrowing of hell and the
Resurrection, B 7.83; John the
Baptist the greatest prophet,
B 14.161-69; Christ as prophet,
CHI 12.190, CHI 33.494; prophecies
of Mary, CHI 13.192-94; acts of the
prophets, CHI 36.540; pagan
prophecies of Christ, CHII 1.214-66,

Supp 1.113-44; the Sybil,
CHII 1.219-22; prophets signified by
vineyard workers, CHII 5.50-72;
prophets in hell, CHII 5.143-60;
St Benedict's gift of,
CHII 11.219-301; prophets signified
by messengers sent to summon
guests to a feast, CHII 23.24-28;
strengthens against tribulations to
come, CHII 37.21-29; false
prophets, LS 15.115-26,
LS 18.94-141, LS 31.842-44,
Supp 18.383-96; prophets signified
by messengers sent to vineyard,
Supp 3.115-23; Israel's persecution
of, Supp 3.119-23; prophets sowers
of seed, Supp 5.247-64; Old
Testament prophets inspired by the
Holy Spirit, Supp 7.52-72; devils
can prophesy, Supp 29.97-104;
Caiaphas' unwitting prophecy of the
Passion, V 1.7-18 (Vf 1.49-61).

PROSTITUTION: *see also*
FORNICATION, SEXUALITY; female
saints sent to houses of,
LS 7.141-76, LS 8.9-17,
LS 9.81-150, LS 35.247-49;
prostitutes who practice infanticide,
Supp 11.379-80; women forced into,
W 20EI.85-91.

PUNISHMENT: *see* THE DAMNED,
HELL, LAW, THE LAW OF MOSES,
OBEDIENCE, SIN, THE SINFUL.

PURGATORY: *see also* THE
DAMNED, HELL, INTERCESSION,
PURITY, REPENTANCE, SIN, THE

SINFUL; general expositions, Supp 11.185-90, 208-42, W 4.29-33; Drihthelm's vision of, CHII 21.21-33, 69-77.

PURITY: *see also* THE BODY, CELIBACY, CONTINENCE, MARRIAGE, SEXUALITY, THE SOUL; the Purification of Mary, **CHI 9,** Supp 11.20-27, Supp 11a.94-10, **V 17 (Vs 17);** impurity signified by unclean animals, CHI 9.138; signified by dove, CHI 9.142; necessary to prayer, V 14.99-111 (Vs 14.79-89); the chosen purified like gold, V 22.81-83 (Vs 22.66-67), W 4.33-36 all men in need of, W 4.24-26; purification of souls in purgatory, W 4.29-33;.

R

RAVEN: *see also* ANIMALS, BIRDS; feeds Elijah, CHII 10.103-106; St Cuthbert repels with a word, CHII 10.184-200.

REASON: *see also* INTELLECT, MEMORY, PHILOSOPHY, THE SOUL; its purpose, CHI 6.96, LS 1.107-109, Supp 16.49-54; the darkness of the mind, CHI 8.132; insufficiency of, CHI 20.286, CHI 24.344; helps man to resemble the Trinity, CHI 20.288-90; animals lack, CHI 21.302, LS 1.96-100, 148-49, V 4.77-82 (Vf 4.87-92); understanding signified by money, CHII 38.49-52; soul killed by loss of, LS 1.146-48; the soul rational, the spirit not, LS 1.188-95; its abuse, Supp 16.55-71; and wisdom, V 20.159-63 (Vs 20.G18-G21).

RELICS: *see also* HEALING, MIRACLES, ROGATIONTIDE, SAINTS; mould of Christ's footprints, B 11.127; St Michael's footprints, B 17.203-205, CHI 34.506; St Martin's clothing, B 18.223, CHII 34.213-16, 264-66; in processions, CHI 18.246, V 12.28-34 (Vs 12.23-27); St John the Baptist's head, CHI 18.246; and miracles, CHI 20.292, CHI 32.486; and healing, CHI 31.474; St Stephen's cloak, CHII 2.13-21; St Basil makes a relic out of miraculous eucharist, LS 3.120-31; veil from St Agatha's tomb stills eruption of Mt Aetna, LS 8.217-34; bones of forty martyred soldiers, LS 11.259-77; translations of saints' bodies, LS 20.70-106, LS 21.21-142; St Æthelthryth's coffin and shroud, LS 20.113-19; healings at St Swithun's tomb, LS 21.95-222, 265-401; St Oswald's head and arm, LS 26.98-102, 162-93; other relics of St Oswald, LS 26.194-268; the true cross, LS 27.6-13, 143-50; disagreements over disposition of St Martin's remains, LS 31.1441-84; gratuitous viewing of punished, LS 32.231-38; veneration of, V 12.72-74 (Vs 12.58-59).

REPENTANCE: *see also*
CONFESSION, FASTING, FORGIVENESS,
HEALING, INTERCESSION, LENT,
ROGATIONTIDE, SIN; general
expositions, CHI 24.340-42, 348-50,
CHI 33.498-50, CHI 39.604,
CHII 9.115-63, LS 12.145-79,
Supp 6.292-301, V 2.103-106
(Vf 2.134-37), **V 3 (Vf 3)**,
V 4.57-71 (Vf 4.65-81),
V 10.248-54 (Vs 10.186-90),
V 19.49-57 (Vs 19.40-47), **V 14
(Vs 14), V 22 (Vs 22), W 11**;
consists of confession and
amendment, B 2.25, B 5.61,
CHI 9.140, CHI 19.268; God's
mercy toward penitents, B 10.107,
CHII 25.35-45, Supp 6.301-12,
Supp 13.72-77; futile after death,
CHI 19.272, V 14.62-77
(Vs 14.51-61); and baptism,
CHI 20.292; requires good works,
CHI 28.412-14; no sin too great for,
CHI 33.498; and the sin against the
Holy Spirit, CHI 33.498-500;
signified by mourners in the
beatitudes, CHI 36.550; signified by
bitter herbs at Passover,
CHII 15.269-72; and despair,
CHII 19.54-59; signified by trees,
CHII 26.101-10; contrasted with
self-righteousness, CHII 28.1-63;
and prayer, CHII 28.44-55; and
ashes, LS 12.33-40; of Ninevites,
LS 13.273-86; of criminals,
LS 19.181-87; Martin offers the
devil opportunity of, LS 31.726-48;
no sin too great for, Supp 6.213-16,
292-312; of heretics, Supp 6.221-27;

the Holy Spirit pities the penitent,
Supp 6.276-77; sickbed repentance,
Supp 11.195-99; God preserves the
disobedient for, Supp 13.48-53;
deathbed repentance,
Supp 19.242-49; summons to,
Supp 27.1-14, W 7.135-41,
W 20BH.117-30, W 20C.163-78,
W 20EI.174-201, W 21.4-9;
efficacious only before the day of
judgement, V 4.1-4 (Vf 4.1-4),
V 15.66-70 (Vs 15.53-56), 92-112
(73-88), V 21.168-70
(Vs 21.130-31), 202-206 (173-76);
during lent, W 14.8-11, 25-36; rites
of, W 15.45-69; contemporary
reluctance to perform,
W 20EI.166-73.

RESURRECTION (GENERAL):
see also THE BODY, DEATH, THE
RESURRECTION OF CHRIST, THE SOUL;
narrations and general expositions,
B 7.95, B 10.109-11, CHI 1.26-28,
CHI 8.132, CHI 14.218,
CHI 16.236-38, CHI 27.396,
CHI 35.532, CHI 40.616,
CHII 37.113-22, CHII 39.125-36,
Supp 2.109-14, **Supp 6**,
Supp 7.156-61, Supp 11.243-60,
297-319, 332-42, Supp 18.418-38,
V 8.32-39 (Vf 8.36-44),
V 21.129-33 (Vs 21.100-102),
W 3.61-65, W 7.95-103; all will rise
regardless of the manner of their
deaths, B 7.95, Supp 11.332-38,
V 2.13-15 (Vf 2.15-17),
V 21.172-74 (Vs 21.132-34); Simon
Magus fakes, B 15.183, CHI 26.370;

the body immortal after,
CHII 31.55-59; signified by the
rising of the wise and foolish virgins,
CHII 39.132-36; signified by spring
foliage, LS 12.29-32; in the books of
the Maccabees, LS 25.471-80;
preservation of saints' bodies an
indication of, LS 32.247-54;
persistence of gender after,
Supp 11.313-19; all will appear fully
grown, regardless of age at death,
Supp 12.109-11.

THE RESURRECTION OF
CHRIST: *see also* EASTER, THE
HARROWING OF HELL, THE PASSION,
RESURRECTION (GENERAL);
narrations and general expositions,
B 7.89-91, CHI 15.220-28, **CHI 16,**
Supp 7.116-61, Supp 9.158-62,
Supp 11.40-45, V 5.134-38
(Vf 5.151-55), W 7.69-74; signified
by the meaning of 'Galilee',
CHI 15.224.

RIGHT: *see also* LEFT; the right
side of St Peter's boat signifies men
of the next world, CHII 16.153-63;
signifies good, Supp 14.167-75.

THE RIGHTEOUS: *see also* THE
BLESSED, CHRISTIANS, THE DAMNED,
THE SINFUL; purified in the
tribulations of the last days,
CHI pref.6, W 4.24-36; the gulf
between the righteous and the sinful,
CHI 19.262; will become like
angels, CHI 19.264; the sufferings
of, CHI 31.472-74, CHI 32.486,

CHI 37.566, V 22.25-36
(Vs 22.21-29); must tolerate the
sinful, CHI 35.526-28; signified by a
vineyard, CHII 5.42-50;
righteousness a virtue of the soul,
LS 1.155-67; the prayer of the
righteous heeded, LS 13.38-49;
blessings of, LS 16.88-93; the
transfiguration of a righteous soul,
V 4.153-61 (Vf 4.170-80).

RIVERS: *see also* SEA, WATER;
signify the gospels, LS 15.173-77;
offerings to springs, LS 17.129-35;
the Jordan stopped flowing at
Christ's baptism, V 16.61-69
(Vs 16.46-52).

ROCK: *see* STONE.

ROGATIONTIDE: *see also*
FASTING, PRAYER, RELICS,
REPENTANCE; observance of,
Supp 11.46-53, Supp 11a.153-61,
V 12.12-21 (Vs 12.10-17), 28-37
(23-29), V 19.58-62 (Vs 19.47-50),
88-94 (71-75), 160-64 (125-29),
V 20.1-5 (Vs 20.1-4); origins of,
V 11.1-8 (Vs 11.1-8), V 12.1-21
(Vs 12.1-17), V 19.149-64
(Vs 19.117-29); repentance during,
V 13.10-18 (Vs 13.10-16);
absolution during, V 19.81-88
(Vs 19.65-71); fasts during,
V 19.95-103 (Vs 19.75-81).

ROSE: *see also* FLOWERS; symbol
of martyrdom, CHI 30.444,
LS 34.72-77, 100-109; symbol of

Christ's blood, LS 34.112-13.

ROYALTY: *see* KINGS.

RUNES: *see also* DIVINATION, SORCERY; as loosing charms, CHII 21.140-80.

S

THE SABBATH: *see also* THE JEWS, SUNDAY; its origin, CHII 12.273-85, Supp 2.211-31; changed to Sunday, CHII 12.300-11, Supp 2.247-55, Supp 18.338-44; signifies Christ in the tomb, CHII 14.327-34; signifies the Passion, Supp 2.247-50; signifies Christian life, Supp 2.256-62; controversy over Christ healing during, Supp 2.262-75.

SACRIFICE: *see* ANIMALS, CHRIST, THE CROSS, THE PASSION.

SAINTS: *see also* MARTYRDOM, PERSECUTION, SORCERY, TORTURE [appendix 1: individual saints by name]; general expositions, **CHI 36**; animals do not harm, CHI 6.102, CHI 32.486-88, CHII 33.175-88, LS 4.399-407, LS 23b.761-95, LS 24.40-57, LS 30.413-20, LS 35.253-306, LS 37.231-49; intercession of, CHI 11.174, CHI 36.546, CHI 37.556, LS 21.284-89, V 12.37-42 (Vs 12.30-34); signified by animal hides, CHII 15.306-309; St Martin

exposes a false saint, CHII 34.133-46; to be praised after their deaths, CHII 38.213-28; not all things in the *Vita Patrum* to be revealed to the laity, LS pref.9-14; serve God as servants attend a king, LS pref.53-68; contemporary men and women cannot match the achievements of, LS 12.279-88; their contempt for the world, LS 28.157-64; their begetting, Supp 1.391-402; the communion of, W 7.88-93.

SALT: signifies teachers, CHII 36.131-37; signifies wisdom, W 8b.22-25, W 8c.53-56.

SALVATION: *see also* THE BLESSED, THE HARROWING OF HELL, HEAVEN; devil forfeits his legal claim to fallen humankind and/or the damned, B 7.85-87, CHI 1.26, CHI 14.216, CHI 20.292, Supp 10.197-203; God's gift, CHII 35.63-70; restoration to life in heaven, V 10.25-44 (Vs 10.20-33).

SCORPION: *see also* ANIMALS; signifies apostasy, CHI 18.252.

SCRIPTURE: *see also* THE JEWS, THE LAW OF MOSES, PARABLES, THE PENTATEUCH, PROPHECY, TEACHING; the devil quotes falsely, B 3.29, CHI 11.170; Christ uses to defeat the devil, B 3.33; men must study, B 10.111; signified by water, CHII 4.52-54; Christ gives an

example of explicating,
CHII 6.33-37; Jewish and Christian
approaches to contrasted,
CHII 8.104-19; St Gregory's study
of, CHII 9.22-31; the Old Testament,
CHII 12.1-6, 255-61,
Supp 3.155-61; the New Testament,
CHII 4.306-16, CHII 12.255-61,
Supp 3.155-61; gospels signified by
numbers fed in miracle of the fish
and loaves, CHII 25.134-37;
perseverance in attending to gospel
teaching, CHII 25.138-43; the four
evangelists signified by the four
beasts of Ezekiel's vision,
CHII 28.64-70; apocryphal gospels,
LS 15.111-26; provenance of the
gospels, LS 15.127-73; signified by
rivers, LS 15.173-77; evangelists
signified by four creatures,
LS 15.178-214; St Mary of Egypt
learns miraculously, LS 23b.585-97
the Old and New Testaments
signified by two halves of a cloven
hoof, LS 25.61-68; the synoptic
gospels concerned with Christ's
humanity, Supp 1.17-19; St John's
gospel concerned with Christ's
divinity, Supp 1.20-26; the gospels
signified by Christ's forty-day fast,
Supp 2.158-66; the meaning of
godspel, Supp 8.1-19; the gospels
signified by Augustus' taxation
edict, V 5.45-52 (Vf 5.52-60);
hearing the gospels confers
forgiveness, V 10.1-8 (Vs 10.1-7);
signified by honey, V 19.79-80
(Vs 19.63-64); reading a cure for
sloth, V 20.110-13 (Vs 20.87-89);

the gospel to be preached throughout
the world before its end, W 2.57-60.

THE SEA: *see also* FISH,
FISHERMEN, RIVERS, SHIP, WATER;
dries up on the day of judgement,
B 7.91; acknowledged Christ,
CHI 7.108, V 16.75-80
(Vs 16.57-61); signifies the world,
CHI 12.182-84, CHII 16.142-52,
CHII 24.86-92, 215-29,
Supp 14.57-62; undersea church of
St Clement, CHI 37.564-66;
St Cuthbert prays in, CHII 10.78-94;
seacoast signifies heaven,
CHII 16.142-52, Supp 14.63-65;
waves signify the sinful,
CHII 24.144-49; signifies
faithlessness, Supp 17.67-72; God's
might deeper than, V 5.197
(Vf 5.221-22); proportion of sea to
dry land, V 9.144-50
(Vs 9.E16-E21).

SEAL: *see also* ANIMALS; seals
minister to St Cuthbert,
CHII 10.79-94.

SERPENT: *see also* ANIMALS,
DRAGON; Simon Magus' bronze
serpents, B 15.173, CHI 26.376;
signifies deceit, CHI 18.252; Moses'
bronze serpent, CHII 13.237-92,
Supp 20.304-52; signifies sins,
CHII 13.257-92, Supp 20.343-46;
signify wisdom, Supp 16.225-57;
moulting signifies abandoning sin,
Supp 16.235-39.

THE SEVEN SLEEPERS OF
EPHESUS: narrations,
CHII 27.182-231, **LS 23**.

SEXUALITY: *see also* ADULTERY,
THE BODY, CASTRATION, CELIBACY,
CHASTITY, FORNICATION, INCEST,
MARRIAGE, PROSTITUTION,
VIRGINITY, WOMAN; unfallen,
CHI 1.18; the apostles' chastity,
CHI 4.58, CHI 21.308; bestial when
not for the purpose of procreation,
CHI 9.148, CHII 4.25-28,
CHII 6.118-23, CHII 19.170-85;
more perilous to indulge sexually
during a holy season than to break a
fast, CHI 11.178; all human
conception sinful, CHI 13.200;
Christ's chastity, CHI 21.308; kinds
of procreation, CHII 1.59-69,
CHII 19.170-78; bees reproduce
without sex, CHII 1.86-90; exploited
to lead St Benedict's monks astray,
CHII 11.153-70; the two sexes
signified by money, CHII 38.74-76;
a widow tries to seduce St Eugenia,
LS 2.144-222; physical desire
deceitful, LS 2.163-67; Christ as
lover and bridegroom, LS 2.352-66,
LS 7.27-66; celibacy within
marriage, LS 4.1-77; original
purpose of to populate the world,
LS 10.211-17; sex on Ash
Wednesday, LS 12.41-58; St Mary
of Egypt's youthful debauchery,
LS 23b.318-419; monastic
temptation to, LS 32.156-75; gender
will remain after the general
resurrection, Supp 11.313-19;

homosexuality a perversion,
V 7.46-50 (Vf 7.50-55).

SHEEP: *see also* ANIMALS, LAMB,
SHEPHERD; general expositions,
LS 2.98-100; signify Christians,
CHI 17; Adam a lost sheep,
CHI 24.338; signified by the name
'Ananias', CHI 27.390; sellers of
sheep signify false teachers,
CHI 28.412; and goats on the day of
judgement, CHII 7.129-79; Christ's
coming changed heathen from dogs
to sheep, CHII 8.88-98.

SHEPHERD: *see also* SHEEP;
general exposition, **CHI 17**; kings
the shepherds of their subjects,
B 4.45; St Peter the shepherd of the
Church, B 15.17, CHII 16.173-85;
signifies teachers, CHI 2.36,
CHI 17.238, 240, V 5.151-59
(Vf 5.169-78); signifies the apostles,
CHI 7.106; Christ the shepherd,
CHII 13.101-107; 'Samaritan'
means 'shepherd', CHII 13.102-104.

SHIP: *see also* FISH, FISHERMEN,
THE SEA; man guided by the devil
like a broken ship, CHI 19.268;
signifies the Church,
CHII 24.131-39, Supp 14.176-94;
signifies Jewish and gentile
believers, Supp 14.53-60, 75-87;
signifies converts, Supp 14.176-86.

THE SIGN OF THE CROSS: *see*
THE CROSS.

SILENCE: in monasteries,
W 10a.48-50.

SILVER: *see also* GEMS, GOLD,
WEALTH; signifies speech,
CHII 40.238-43; transfigured body
of the blessed likened to, V 4.158-59
(Vf 4.176-77).

SIN: *see also* CONFESSION,
COVETOUSNESS, DESPAIR, THE FALL
OF ADAM AND EVE, THE FALL OF
ANGELS, FORGIVENESS,
FORNICATION, GLUTTONY, PRIDE,
REPENTANCE, THE SINFUL, SLOTH,
TEMPTATION, VAINGLORY, WRATH;
original, B 2.17, CHI 9.144,
CHI 10.154, CHII 1.110-20,
CHII 19.291-94, Supp 11.499-501,
Supp 12.134-38, V 16.24-47
(Vs 16.19-35), V 21.126-29
(Vs 21.97-101), W 8b.19-21,
W 8c.32-34; equated with blindness,
B 2.17-19, CHI 10.154; four modes
of, B 3.35; four seasons of, B 3.35;
lesser and greater, B 3.37-39,
CHI 24.340, CHI 32.484,
CHII 40.250-72; men must be
instructed about their variety,
B 4.43; the deceits of the devil,
B 5.55; sinful pleasures transitory,
B 5.59; signified by the stone on
Lazarus' tomb, B 6.75; revealed on
the day of judgement, B 10.109-11,
V 8.9-26 (Vf 8.10-29), V 9.1-15
(Vs 9.1-13); children not responsible
for parents', CHI 7.114; unconfessed
sins a cause of death and disease,
CHI 8.124, CHI 16.284,

CHI 34.604; signified by the crowds
who tried to silence blind man,
CHI 10.156; Christ's sinlessness,
CHI 11.166; signified by rope,
CHI 14.208; the burden of,
CHI 14.208; apostles' and bishops'
power to forgive, CHI 16.232-34;
consumed by the fire of the Holy
Spirit, CHI 22.320; disease punishes,
CHI 31.470-72; signified by death,
CHI 33.492; enters the gates of the
body, CHI 33.492; and the death of
the soul, CHI 33.496; against the
Holy Spirit, CHI 33.498-500,
Supp 6.217-27, 269-77; abstaining
from is a martyrdom, CHI 36.544;
pride the origin of, CHI 36.550;
signified by fire, CHII 7.114-16,
V 10.129-32 (Vs 10.98-100),
V 20.30-34 (Vs 20.25-28); signified
by nations destroyed by Israel,
CHII 12.477-92, 560-65; catalogues
of, CHII 12.483-541,
CHII 19.285-90, CHII 25.50-53,
CHII 40.261-72, 279-87,
LS 1.99-112, LS 16.267-311,
LS 17.23-28, Supp 4.246-57,
Supp 16.72-83, Supp 19.127-30,
V 2.69-75 (Vf 2.94-100), V 3.19-24
(Vf 3.21-27), V 9L.125-33,
V 10.44-54 (Vs 10.34-41),
V 14.147-51 (Vs 14.117-19),
V 20.22-28 (Vs 20.19-23), 61-140
(50-G3), V 21.219-24
(Vs 21.187-91), W 8c.156-73,
W 10a.10-19, W 10c.62-66, 79-117,
W 13.100-103, W 20BH.86-103,
W 20C.131-44, W 20EI.133-46;
specific sins opposed to correlative

virtues, CHII 12.542-59, V 19.68-80
(Vs 19.54-64), V 20.61-151
(Vs 20.46-G12), W 10c.122-40;
symbolized by snakes,
CHII 13.257-92, Supp 20.343-46;
signified by Egypt, CHII 15.64-68;
signified by fertilizer,
CHII 26.101-10; some too great for
intercessory prayer, CHII 35.123-27;
undermines a teacher's authority,
CHII 36.48-56; distorts God's
creation, CHII 39.198-205; purged
by fire on the day of judgement,
CHII 40.243-58, 272-75; deadly sins
never purged in hell,
CHII 40.258-61; proper object of
anger, LS 1.103-107; rejection of sin
is the beauty of the soul,
LS 1.153-55; requires consent of the
will, LS 9.84-93, refraining from is
the true fasting, LS 13.111-15,
Supp 2.167-76; equated with death,
Supp 6.137-42; consumed in
purgatory Supp 11.225-28; suffering
in hell proportional to,
Supp 11.493-96; renunciation of
signified by a snake shedding its
skin, Supp 16.235-39; devils show
sick man a book of his sins,
Supp 19.136-207; signified by
arrows, V 4.308-21 (Vf 4.340-54);
pollutes the earth, W 3.27-29; men
afflicted for during the last days,
W 5.14-19; Isaiah's vision of
Israel's, W 11.99-117; blinds the
nation, W 11.169-74; bishops will
be punished for the sins they failed to
chastise, W 17.41-68; contemporary
woes a punishment for,

W 20BH.9-22, W 20C.15-24,
W 20EI.14-23; sins of the Britons in
the time of Gildas, W 20EI.176-86.

SINCERITY: *see* HONESTY.

THE SINFUL: *see also* THE
BLESSED, THE DAMNED, DEATH, THE
FALL OF ADAM AND EVE, HELL, THE
RIGHTEOUS, SIN, TEMPTATION; are
the devil's limbs, B 3.33,
CHI 11.168; types of, B 5.61,
CHI 8.132, CHII 19.285-90,
LS 17.34-44, Supp 11.375-83,
V 4.31-51 (Vf 4.35-58), V 21.18-28
(Vs 21.14-22), W 7.128-35,
W 13.92-97, W 20EI.160-66;
ugliness of the sinful soul,
CHI 8.122-24; see the wounded
Christ on the day of judgement,
CHI 15.222-24, V 2.15-19
(Vf 2.18-22); angels hostile toward,
CHI 15.222; the gulf between the
sinful and the righteous, CHI 19.262;
mutual flattery of, CHI 33.492-94;
sinners like the dead burying the
dead, CHI 33.492-94; toleration of,
CHI 35.526-28; signified by fish
escaped from St Peter's net,
CHII 16.163-67, Supp 14.126-39;
damned by pride, CHII 23.84-94;
saved by humility, CHII 23.84-94;
signified by the waves under Christ's
feet, CHII 24.144-49; Christ came
for, CHII 32.67-75; God does not
hear the prayers of, CHII 35.118-19;
good will toward, CHII 35.119-23;
all creation makes war on,
CHII 37.52-65, W 3.29-44; signified

by slack servants, CHII 38.99-111; punishment of, LS 16.88-93; sinfulness a kind of idolatry, LS 17.49-51; God's patience with, LS 23b.384-91; signified by blindness, Supp 1.294-98; signified by dogs, Supp 13.228-32; signified by swine, Supp 13.232-34; remain unrepentant on the day of judgement, V 2.10-12 (Vf 2.12-14), the folly of, V 2.20-34 (Vf 2.23-40); narration of the judgement of a sinful soul, V 4.194-307 (Vf 4.214-339); futile remorse of on the day of judgement, V 21.168-70 (Vs 21.130-31), 202-206 (173-76); terrible death of, V 22.1-25 (Vs 22.1-20); are Antichrist's limbs, W 1b.12-15; harm themselves by taking the eucharist, W 8c.45-52; shunning of, W 21.26-31.

SLANDER: *see also* DECEIT; a kind of murder, B 5.65; condemned, W 11.156-61.

SLAVERY: St Paul's admonitions to servants and masters, CHI 26.378; St Gregory's encounter with English slaves, CHII 9.49-80; relations between servants and masters, CHII 19.215-27; bondage to sin, CHII 35.34-62; slaves ennobled by service to Christian masters, LS 2.84-87; runaway slaves restored to masters signify men subjected to Christ, V 5.70-76 (Vf 5.82-90); to the heathen, W 20BH.75-81, W 20C.87-92, W 20EI.83-85;

runaway slaves kill without paying wergild, W 20C.97-103, W 20EI.100-106; slaves enslave their erstwhile lords, W 20C.115-18, W 20EI.117-19.

SLEEP: the seven sleepers of Ephesus, CHII 27.182-231, LS 23; likened to death, CHII 39.92-104.

SLOTH: *see also* GOOD WORKS, SIN; general expositions, CHII 12.519-24, 555, V 20.104-13 (Vs 20.82-89); innocence sometimes confused with, CHII 3.179; renunciation of signified by Christ's command to bedridden man to rise, Supp 2.186-91; harms the soul, V 7.60-71 (Vf 7.65-78); besetting sin of monks, V 20.106-108 (Vs 20.83-85); consequences of, V 20.108-10 (Vs 20.85-87); remedied by reading, good works, and a desire for heaven, V 20.110-13 (Vs 20.87-89).

SNAKE: *see* SERPENT.

SNOW: gentleness of, CHI 15.222-24.

SOCIETY: St Paul's prescriptions for, CHI 26.378; men must support one another like stones in a wall, CHII 40.125-29; God will bless if clergy and laity observe their obligations, LS 13.133-38; God punishes for leaders' misbehaviour, LS 13.139-46; dissolution during last days, LS 13.294-311; orders of, LS 25.812-22; contemporary collapse of, W 20BH.56-75, W 20C.61-83, W 20EI.53-83.

SOLOMON'S TEMPLE: *see* THE TEMPLE OF SOLOMON.

SORCERERS: *see* SORCERY.

SORCERY: *see also* ASTROLOGY, CURSING, DIVINATION, HEALING, IDOLATRY, PROPHECY, RUNES; general expositions, LS 21.464-98; sorcerers' torments in hell, B 5.61, V 4.45-48 (Vf 4.50-55); Simon Magus, **B 15**, CHI 26.370-82, LS 17.118-21; among the Myrmedonians, B 19.229; healing spells, CHI 31.474-76; Hermoines, CHII 27.6-107; Zaraos and Arfaxath, CHII 32.80-142, CHII 33.1-259; love charms, LS 3.358-402; saints accused of, LS 4. 146-48, LS 6.186-213, LS 7.177-83, 207-10, 240-43, LS 11.109-19, LS 24.58-67, LS 35.152-57, 173-87; sorcerers cannot afflict saints, LS 9.103-106, LS 14.48-81; witchcraft, LS 17.67-83; casting of lots permissible if done in faith, LS 17.84-87; against augury, LS 17.88-91; and the devil, LS 17.108-13; pharaoh's magicians LS 17.114-17, Supp 1.258-66, Supp 4.139-44; not to be resorted to for healing, LS 17.122-28; defeated by the sign of the cross,

LS 21.469-98; false monks practice, LS 31.792-830; Saul and the witch of Endor, **Supp 29**; deceits of, Supp 29.1-35; dead cannot be raised by, Supp 29.50-65, 118-23.

SORROW: *see also* SUFFERING; signified by pigeon and dove, CHI 9.142.

THE SOUL: *see also* THE BODY, REASON; its relation to the body: B 2.21, CHI 10.158-60, CHI 14.218, CHI 19.264, CHII 31.40-49, LS 1.176-225, LS 17.1-15, Supp 2.105-108, Supp 6.143-59, Supp 11.216-19, 243-60, 481-86, V 4.117-307 (Vf 4.131-339), V 7.94-108 (Vf 7.102-18), V 9.68-82 (Vs 9.54-64), V 22.147-50 (Vs 22.117-19), 157-63 (125-29); fed by spiritual instruction, B 5.57, CHI 11.166, LS 13.89-90; rejoined with the body on the day of judgement, B 5.57, CHI 20.294, V 4.162-83 (Vf 4.180-202); its immortality, B 5.57-59, CHI 1.16, CHI 6.96, CHII 31.50-59; care of, **B 8**, V 14.1-17 (Vs 14.1-14), 45-53 (37-43), 86-98 (69-79); neglect of during the last days, B 10.109; men will answer to God with, B 10.113, CHI 2.36; of Mary, B 13.147-57; animals lack, CHI 1.16, CHI 6.96, CHI 20.276, CHI 21.302, CHII 19.178-81, LS 1.25-28, 96-100, 148-49, LS 17.241-52, V 4.77-82 (Vf 4.87-92); nature of,

CHI 1.20, CHI 10.158-60,
LS 1.81-239; implanted in the
womb, CHI 1.20; of the sinful,
CHI 8.122, CHI 10.160,
CHII 8.34-44, V 22.37-42
(Vs 22.30-34); reconciled with the
body in heaven, CHI 19.272;
resembles God, CHI 20.288;
resembles the Trinity,
CHI 20.288-90; has no
pre-existence, CHI 20.292,
CHII 12.294-96, Supp 2.229-31;
devils attack and seize at death,
CHI 28.414, Supp 27.15-47, 83-105;
death of, CHI 33.496,
CHII 20.180-83, Supp 6.160-212;
the seat of wisdom, CHI 35.520;
winged with love, CHII 19.85-90;
fought over by angels and devils at
death, CHII 20.57-92, 111-51;
virtues of, LS 1.55-71, V 20.152-79
(Vs 20.G13-G33), V 21.61-86
(Vs 21.48-67); its function is to love
its origin, LS 1.92-96; its three-fold
nature, LS 1.96-100; its swiftness,
LS 1.122-31; its ceaseless activity,
LS 1.131-36, 216-25; the soul is to
the body as God is to the soul,
LS 1.141-46, 205-208; killed by loss
of reason, LS 1.146-48; lost its
blessedness but not its immortality in
the fall, LS 1.150-53; its beauty
consists of its rejection of sin,
LS 1.153-55; names of,
LS 1.180-88; and the spirit,
LS 1.188-95; guides the five senses,
LS 1.195-96; adorned by good
works, LS 1.208-14; is not breath,
LS 1.214-16; made beautiful by love

of wisdom, LS 1.225-39; Adam's
curse did not apply to, LS 12.27-28;
fruits of the spirit, LS 17.52-59;
hellfire burns, Supp 11.478-92;
harmed by sloth, V 7.60-71
(Vf 7.65-78); its acts exposed at
death, V 9.59-65 (Vs 9.47-52);
absolute sundering from body after
death, V 9.65-82 (Vs 9.53-64);
judgement of, V 10.55-121
(Vs 10.42-91); equated with thought,
V 22.152-56 (Vs 22.121-24).

SPEECH: *see* CURSING, DECEIT,
LANGUAGE, OATHS, POETRY,
SLANDER.

SPIRIT: *see* LIFE, THE SOUL.

STARS: *see also* ASTROLOGY, THE
HEAVENS, THE MOON, THE MORNING
STAR, THE SUN; on the day of
judgement, B 7.91-93, V 2.6-7
(Vf 2.7-8), V 15.56-57 (Vs 15.46),
V 21.164-65 (Vs 21.126-27);
creation of, CHI 6.100; the star of
Bethlehem, CHI 7.106, 108,
CHI 15.228; not arbiters of fate,
CHI 7.110; honoured Christ,
CHI 7.108-110; during the last days,
CHI 40.608-10; transformed after
the day of judgement,
CHI 40.616-18; worship of,
Supp 21.85-86, W 12.21-22;
transfigured body of the blessed
likened to, V 4.160 (Vf 4.178);
God's might brighter than, V 5.197
(Vf 5.222); will fall on account of
men's sins, W 3.43-44; falling stars

signify apostates, W 3.50-53.

STONE: signifies Christ, CHI 6.98,
CHI 7.106, CHII 12.215-20,
CHII 15.179-81, CHII 40.93-96;
signifies heart hardened against the
good, CHI 18.252, CHII 6.79-89,
CHII 12.250-54, CHII 13.221-36,
Supp 19.30-33; signifies St Peter,
CHI 26.368; signifies faith,
CHI 26.368; stones of fallen temple
signify wicked deeds, CHI 28.410;
signifies heart strengthened against
evil, CHII 4.55-57; signifies the
Church, CHII 24.162-72; believers
the stones of the Church,
CHII 40.108-10; men must support
one another like stones in a wall,
CHII 40.125-29; offerings to,
LS 17.129-35; recognized Christ,
V 16.82-85 (Vs 16.62-65).

STORMS: sent to punish sin,
W 3.38-40.

STUPIDITY: *see* INTELLECT,
MEMORY, REASON.

SUFFERING: *see also* DEATH,
DISEASE, FAMINE, HELL,
MARTYRDOM, PERSECUTION,
TORTURE; God permits,
CHI 31.472-74, CHI 32.486,
CHI 37.566, CHII 37.202-205,
LS 17.174-212, V 22.81-83
(Vs 22.66-67), W 4.17-24; some use
wealth to avoid, LS 12.100-19; pain
in this life a foretaste of hell,
V 9.84-89 (Vs 9.66-70); is

temporary in this world, V 22.67-80
(Vs 22.55-65); is permanent in the
next world, V 22.89-95
(Vs 22.72-76), W 3.65-73; punishes
sin, W 3.9-10, W 20BH.9-22,
48-56, W 20C.15-28, 61-69,
106-14, 127-31, W 20EI.12-23,
48-61, 129-33.

SUICIDE: *see also* DEATH;
St Martin raises a suicide from
death, B 18.219, CHII 34.105-109,
LS 31.239-53, V 18.124-38
(Vs 18.C9-C19); suicides damned,
LS 19.229-30; suicides on the day of
judgement, V 8.39-42 (Vf 8.44-47).

THE SUN: *see also* THE HEAVENS,
THE MOON, STARS; on the day of
judgement, B 7.91, 93,
Supp 11.287-89, V 2.6-7 (Vf 2.7-8),
V 15.57 (Vs 15.46-47), V 21.164-65
(Vs 21.126-27); signifies Christ,
B 14.163, CHI 30.444,
Supp 1.420-26; acknowledged Christ
as the Creator, CHI 7.108,
CHII 33.235-53, LS 29.9-13;
analogy for the Trinity,
CHI 20.282-86, LS 1.70-81; analogy
for God's omnipresence,
CHI 20.286-88; worship of,
CHI 26.366, Supp 21.82-84,
W 12.17-21; eclipse of,
CHI 40.608-10; during the last days,
CHI 40.608-10; transformed after
the day of judgement,
CHI 40.616-18, Supp 11.513-16,
Supp 21.62-65; stood still for
Joshua, CHII 12.398-406, 565-71;

signifies God, CHII 30.26-30; lost its brightness after the fall of Adam and Eve, Supp 21.56-61; first day of the week named for, Supp 21.166-70; transfigured body of the blessed likened to, V 4.160-61 (Vf 4.178-80); shone at midnight on Christ's nativity, V 6.22-25 (Vf 6.25-29); men will shine like on the day of judgement, V 8.90-92 (Vf 8.99-102); grows dark to punish sin, W 3.41-42; the sun darkened signifies God's hiding his power during the reign of Antichrist, W 3.45-48.

SUNDAY: *see also* THE SABBATH; its distinctions, B 12.133; sabbath changed to, CHII 12.300-11, Supp 2.247-55, Supp 18.338-44; men should not kneel on, LS 12.3-7; obligation to honour, Supp 16.78-81; named for the sun, Supp 21.166-70.

SWEARING: *see* CURSING, OATHS.

SWINE: *see also* ANIMALS; the Gadarene swine, CHII 23.147-94, LS 17.190-98; signify backsliders, CHII 23.177-94; signify sinners, Supp 13.233-34, Supp 17.260-71.

THE SYBIL: *see* PROPHECY.

T

TAXATION: *see also* ALMSGIVING, TITHING, WEALTH; Christ's attitude toward, CHI 34.510-12;

taxgathering a dishonest trade, CHII 16.130-42; by Augustus, V 5.10-16 (Vf 5.11-17); signifies man's debt to Christ, V 5.87-99 (Vf 5.101-15); church tolls, W 13.70-79.

TEACHERS: *see* TEACHING.

TEACHING: *see also* PARABLES, PHILOSOPHY, PROPHECY, SCRIPTURE; general expositions, **CHII 36**, **W 16b**; spiritual instruction feeds the soul, B 5.57, CHI 11.168, LS 13.89-90; teachers' duties, B 6.81, CHII 19.107-16, 120-26, Supp 15.164-77, Supp 18.169-79, W 6.1-20, W 8b.1-13, W 8c.1-10, **W 16b**; St Paul the Church's teacher, B 15.171; contemporary dearth of, CHI pref.6; teacher's pronouncements signified by Augustus' edict, CHI 2.34; teachers signified by shepherds, CHI 2.36, CHI 17.238, V 5.151-59 (Vf 5.169-78); teachers signified by angels, CHI 2.36; signified by bread, CHI 11.168, CHI 19.264-66, CHII 25.110-20, Supp 19.1-9; signified by fish, CHII 25.111-12; teachers signified by two disciples sent to fetch an ass, CHI 14.206; preaching of the gospel signified by untying an animal, CHI 14.208; signified by those who gathered palms on Palm Sunday, CHI 14.212-14; effects of, CHI 25.362, V 7.1-6 (Vf 7.1-6); false teachers, CHI 28.412,

CHII 3.233-44, CHII 20.183-85, Supp 4.209-11, W 2.54-55, W 16b.11-29; the honour of, CHI 36.548, teachers signified by vineyard workers, CHII 5.48-72; signified by seed, CHII 6.53-89, Supp 5.265-78; signified by a meal, CHII 8.99-104; Christ's example to teachers, CHII 13.145-49; neglect of, CHII 23.63-70, Supp 19.25-30; persistence in receiving, CHII 25.138-43; all teachers of the gospels signified by four creatures in Ezekiel, CHII 28.64-73; a good work, CHII 29.71-82; teachers signified by architects, CHII 36.23-26; signified by lambs, CHII 36.57-62; patience of teachers, CHII 36.57-68; signified by salt, CHII 36.131-37; by example, CHII 38.54-66; a generic eulogy for a dead teacher, CHII 38.213-46; symbolic healing, CHII 38.232-41; its authority not to be appropriated by the unlearned, CHII 40.298-301; not all things in the *Vita Patrum* to be revealed to the laity, LS pref.9-14; St Sebastian teaches from an angel's book, LS 5.89-104; signified by morning, LS 5.105-11; teachers must teach the meaning of the Lord's Prayer and the Creed, LS 12.264-67; reception of dependent upon the inspiration of the Holy Spirit, Supp 10.105-19; teachers must have learning and righteousness, Supp 13.128-33; Christ as teacher, Supp 13.134-45, Supp 14.49-52; teachers signified by

fishermen, Supp 14.66-74; teachers are stewards, Supp 16.274-83; signified by farmwork, Supp 18.141-99; teachers signified by ploughmen, Supp 18.153-68; teachers signified by dogs, Supp 18.175-79, W 16b.23-26; signified by milk, Supp 19.1-9; signified by water, Supp 19.30-33; wilful ignorance of, Supp 20.401-10; teachers signified by lamps, V 11.9-20 (Vs 11.9-17); must warn of approaching disaster, W 1b.25-34; hypocrisy of teachers during the last days, W 5.20-22; in monasteries, W 10a.43-45; a bishop's teaching should be followed rather than his example, W 17.68-74; contemporary defiance of, W 20BH.44-47.

THE TEMPLE OF SOLOMON: *see also* THE JEWS [appendix 2: JERUSALEM]; general expositions, **CHII 40**, W 18.6-33, 66-69, 91-123; rending of the veil at the Crucifixion, CHII 14.276-77, 295-98; St James martyred in, CHII 17.91-104; Judas Maccabeus cleanses, LS 25.378-84; signified by tower in vineyard parable, Supp 3.83-105; Jewish prayer in, Supp 5.190-93.

TEMPTATION: of Christ, **B 3**, **CHI 11**, Supp 11.28-32, Supp 11a.128-32, V 12.21-28 (Vs 12.17-22); of Eve, CHI 1.16-18; necessary for full growth,

CHI 11.170, CHI 19.268; three kinds of, CHI 11.174-76; of Adam, CHI 11.176-78; God tempts no one, CHI 19.268; resistance to, CHI 19.268; signified by Israel's trials in the wilderness, CHII 12.192-95.

THE TEN COMMANDMENTS: *see* THE LAW OF MOSES.

THIEVES: at the Crucifixion, CHI 37.576, CHII 5.122-42, CHII 14.249-62, LS 19.161-71; theft in the Decalogue, CHII 12.325-26; capital punishment for, LS 19.178-80, LS 32.214-30; repentance of, LS 19.181-87; and the devil, LS 19.188-93; Isaiah's condemnation of, W 11.118-24; Mercury a thief, W 12.65-72.

THORNS: symbol of wealth, CHII 6.37-43; signify Adam's curse, CHII 14.213-18, CHII 26.42-47.

THE THREE KINGS: *see* THE MAGI.

THE THREE WISE MEN: *see* THE MAGI.

TIDES: *see also* THE SEA; the moon affects, CHI 6.102.

TIME: *see* DAY, DAYS OF THE WEEK, NEW YEAR, NIGHT, THE SABBATH, TIDES.

TITHING: *see also* ALMSGIVING, POVERTY, TAXATION, WEALTH; general expositions, **B 4**, CHI 11.178, Supp 30.75-114, V 20.28-30 (Vs 20.23-25), W 13.70-79, W 14.11-15; signified by lent amounting to one-tenth of a year, B 3.35, CHI 11.178; contemporary failure of, W 3.29-38; during lent, W 14.11-15.

TORTURE: *see also* CONVERSION, THE CROSS, HELL, THE PASSION, SUFFERING; by sorcery, B 19.229; by blinding, B 19.229; by dragging, B 19.241-43, LS 14.151-60, LS 15.49-57, 80-89; by stoning, CHI 3.52, LS 11.98-108; by boiling oil, CHI 4.58, CHI 37.574; by fire, CHI 29.424-30, CHII 1.230-66, LS 2.396-99, LS 4.332-40, 389-95, LS 7.216-39, LS 8.166-82, LS 9.116-23, LS 15.90-96, LS 29.241-44, 249-51, LS 30.420-61, LS 35.293-306, LS 37.162-74; by beating, CHI 29.432, LS 4.141-52, LS 14.41-47, LS 19.73-79, LS 22.154-58, 230-44, LS 24.40-48, LS 35.188-93, LS 37.156-74; by drowning, LS 2.389-95; by starvation, LS 2.400-11, LS 22.135-40, LS 37.45-67; by casting into a pit filled with decomposing corpses, LS 4.209-12; by cutting out tongue, LS 25.115, Supp 23.185-97; by boiling water, LS 25.115-19, LS 34.342-51; by crucifixion, CHI 38.594-96,

LS 29.252-55; by wild animals,
LS 4.399-407, LS 24.28-39,
LS 29.245-48, LS 30.413-20; by the
sword, LS 7.240-49; by mutilation
or dismemberment, LS 9.116-33,
LS 14.41-47, LS 23.68-81,
LS 25.115-19; by freezing,
LS 11.140-62; by leg-breaking,
LS 11.235-58; by wheel,
LS 14.85-95; by boiling lead,
LS 14.104-16; by being sown into a
hide, LS 35.158-63; by the rack,
LS 35.311-18, LS 37.94-112; by
burying alive, LS 35.324-40.

THE TOWER OF BABEL: *see
also* LANGUAGE, PENTECOST;
narrations and general expositions,
CHI 1.22-24, CHI 22.318,
Supp 21.72-81, W 12.7-16; and the
confusion of languages, CHI 22.318,
CHII 32.89-105, Supp 21.77-81,
W 12.10-16.

THE TRANSFIGURATION:
narrated, Supp 1.427-33.

TRANSLATION: *see* LANGUAGE,
SCRIPTURE.

TRANSUBSTANTIATION: *see*
THE EUCHARIST.

TREASON: traitors shall perish,
LS 19.194-95, 229-34; of Absalom,
LS 19.196-224; of Judas,
LS 19.225-28; men betray one
another too readily, W 3.18-20,

W 9.120-28; failure of trust in last
days, W 3.53-60, W 20BH.60-71,
W 20C.73-83, W20EI.67-78;
betrayal of one's lord the most
heinous crime, W 20BH.66-67,
W 20C.78-79, W 20EI.71-76.

TREASURE: *see* GEMS, GOLD
SILVER, WEALTH.

TREES: *see also* AGRICULTURE,
FRUIT; signify men, CHII 26.47-100;
signify repentance, CHII 26.101-10;
spring foliage signifies general
resurrection, LS 12.29-32; offerings
to, LS 17.129-35; olive trees,
Supp 16.131-41; signify pride,
V 10.208-18 (Vs 10.156-63).

THE TRINITY: *see also* CHRIST,
THE CREATION, GOD, THE HOLY
SPIRIT, THE INCARNATION; general
expositions, CHI 9.150, CHI 13.196,
CHI 15.228, CHI 20.276-92,
CHI 22.324-26, CHI 31.464-66,
CHI 33.498-500, CHII 3.115-33,
CHII 4.68-78, CHII 12.261-67,
CHII 22.34-58, 68-88, 118-36,
163-72, LS 34.157-70,
Supp 3.176-81, Supp 4.150-72,
Supp 8.185-204, Supp 10.177-80,
Supp 11.83-89, Supp 11a.1-19,
188-230, **V 16 (Vs 16)**, V 19.1-11
(Vs 19.1-9), W 7.26-33,
W 10c.141-46, W 12.89-95; faith in
before the advent of Christ, B 6.81;
at the Creation, CHI 1.10, 13,
CHI 20.278, CHI 26.366-68,
LS 1.14-19, 33-35, LS 16.1-8,

Supp 1.84-97, Supp 6.243-53; signified by bread, CHI 18.248; procession of persons, CHI 19.278-86, Supp 1.155-67, Supp 6.228-42, Supp 9.110-29; the sun an analogy for, CHI 20.282-86, LS 1.70-79; the soul resembles, CHI 20.288-90, LS 1.112-22, LS 34.166-70; signified by Abraham's three visitors, CHII 13.184-90; sustains the obedient, CHII 19.33-35; belief in, LS 1.38-41, LS 16.248-52; signified by a voice crying out three times, LS 10.107-108; signified by the three 'holies' of the *sanctus*, LS 15.215-18; the unity of, Supp 6.266-68; fire an analogy for, V 16.153-65 (Vs 16.120-29); signified by three dips into baptismal waters, W 8b.45-47; signified by three dips into water at christening, W 8c.78-81.

TRUMPET: signifies St John the Baptist, B 14.163.

U

UNBELIEVERS: *see* THE DAMNED, THE HEATHEN, IDOLATRY, THE SINFUL, VIKINGS.

UNDERSTANDING: *see* INTELLECT, MIND, REASON, TEACHING.

UNITY: symbolized by pigeons, CHI 9.142; of the Church,

CHI 9.142, CHI 19.272-74, CHI 26.368, CHII 15.237-44, CHII 40.110-17, W 18.70-74; of the Trinity, Supp 6.266-68.

V

VAINGLORY: *see also* PRIDE, SIN; general expositions, CHII 12.525-31, 556, V 20.125-40 (Vs 20.98-G3); in the temptation of Adam, CHI 11.176; in the temptation of Christ, CHI 11.176-78; vanity in clothing, CHI 23.328-30, V 2.98-103 (Vf 2.128-33); valid boasting, CHII 13.169-83; the evil of boasting, Supp 17.190-202; consequences of, V 20.131-34 (Vs 20.103-104); remedied by the memory of God's goodness, V 20.134-40 (Vs 20.105-G3).

VALLEY: *see also* MOUNTAIN; symbol of humility, CHI 25.362, Supp 5.178-79.

VANITY: *see* CLOTHING, PRIDE, VAINGLORY.

VIGILS: *see also* GOOD WORKS; penitential, V 3.64-83 (Vf 3.71-98); correct observance of, W 18.54-65.

VIKINGS: *see also* THE HEATHEN; oppression of Christians, LS 11.353-56; raids in Northumbria, LS 32.26-132; English apostates reverting to Norse paganism,

Supp 14.126-39; incursions linked
with tribulations of last days,
W 3.20-26; fugitive slaves become,
W 20C.97-103, W 20EI.100-106;
tribute to, W 20C.103-105,
W 20EI.106-109, 119-28; conquest
of England, W 20C.106-14,
W 20EI.109-28.

VINEGAR: *see* WINE.

VINEYARD: *see also*
AGRICULTURE, WINE; parables
explicated, **CHII 5, Supp 3**;
signifies the righteous,
CHII 5.42-50; workers signify
teachers, CHII 5.48-72; signifies
Israel, Supp 3.61-82.

VIRGINITY: *see also* THE BODY,
CELIBACY, CHASTITY, FORNICATION,
MARRIAGE, SEXUALITY; general
expositions, **CHII 39,**
Supp 19.42-89; Mary's perpetual,
B 1.3, B 13.155, CHI 1.24,
CHI 2.34, 42, CHI 4.58,
CHI 13.194, 198-200, CHI 30.438,
CHI 36.546, CHII 1.73-90,
CHII 3.12-13, Supp 1.413-26,
Supp 11a.79-80, V 17.28-46
(Vs 17.23-37), W 6.143-45; of
St John the Evangelist, CHI 4.58,
CHI 30.438; its superiority,
CHI 9.148, CHI 30.444-446,
CHII 4.294-305, CHII 6.131-35,
Supp 19.66-89; of Christ,
CHI 21.308; signified by the lily,
CHI 30.444; of the Church,
CHI 33.492, CHII 39.81-87; Mary's

signified by Aaron's rod,
CHII 1.47-58; of faith,
CHII 39.78-81; within marriage,
LS 4.1-77, LS 20.1-30, 120-35,
LS 34.13-48; angels protect female
saints', LS 7.148-76; the Holy Spirit
promised to the pure, LS 9.72-80;
preserves the body from corruption
after death, LS 20.107-12,
LS 32.164-88; should be voluntary,
Supp 19.48-52.

VIRTUES: *see also* GOOD WORKS;
catalogues of, B 7.95-97,
CHII 8.80-87, LS 13.116-22,
LS 16.246-66, 312-77, V 2.75-83
(Vf 2.101-10), 107-12 (138-44),
V 3.14-17 (Vf 3.15-19), V 4.82-90
(Vf 4.92-100), 102-16 (114-30),
V 9.222-26 (Vs 9.141-44),
V 14.152-62 (Vs 14.121-27),
V 16.184-97 (Vs 16.144-54),
V 19.62-66 (Vs 19.51-53),
V 21.48-56 (Vs 21.38-44), 96-109
(74-84), 224-38 (191-201),
W 10a.19-28, W 10c.67-71, 149-95,
W 13.19-25; Christ establishes,
CHI 9.144; signified by oil,
CHI 15.220-22; are spiritual wealth,
CHII 6.47-52; specific virtues
correlated with analogous sins,
CHII 12.542-59, V 19.68-80
(Vs 19.54-64), V 20.61-151
(Vs 20.46-G12), W 10c.79-117;
signified by a gate, CHII 28.73-82;
signified by gems, CHII 40.181-87,
238-41; the soul grows by increasing
in, LS 1.110-12; virtues and powers
of the soul, LS 1.155-71,

V 20.152-79 (Vs 20.G13-G33), V 21.61-86 (Vs 21.48-67); restraint the mother of, LS 1.163-64; different degrees of virtue, Supp 19.9-14; rewards of, V 4.82-90 (Vf 4.92-100); men must clothe themselves in, V 21.57-61 (Vs 21.45-48)

THE VISIO PAULI: false versions of, CHII 20.1-18.

VOWS: *see* BAPTISM, CURSING, OATHS.

W

WAR: *see also* VIKINGS; during the last days, B 10.107, CHII 37.21-65, V 15.29-31 (Vs 15.23-25); God as a general, CHI 24.342; wars of annihilation permitted in the Old Testament, CHI 35.522, CHII 12.439-45; spiritual warfare, CHII 12.464-92, CHII 25.129-34, LS 25.688-700, 823-62, V 19.66-80 (Vs 19.54-64), W 8b.32-36, W 8c.62-68;Christ forbids fighting on his behalf, CHII 14.107-13; Christian soldiers refuse to obey pagan commanders, CHII 34.45-58, LS 11.26-31, LS 28.8-73, LS 31.98-130; the Maccabean revolt, **LS 25**; wars of Israel signify spiritual striving, LS 25.701-703; kinds of, LS 25.704-14; monks and pacifism, LS 25.823-62; waged upon the heathen by St Eustace, LS 30.294-314; St Martin's

reluctant military service, LS 31.10-36; kings' delegation of military affairs to generals, **Supp 22**; Mars the patron of, Supp 21.126-32, W 12.58-65.

WATER: *see also* THE SEA, RIVER; birds created from, CHI 1.16; signifies the Holy Spirit, CHI 25.362, Supp 5.131-58; sanctified by Christ's baptism, CHII 3.96-98, V 16.16-19 (Vs 16.13-15); signifies scripture, CHII 4.52-54; signifies the Old Testament, CHII 4.306-16; signifies almsgiving, CHII 7.114-16, V 10.129-32 (Vs 10.98-100), V 20.30-34 (Vs 20.25-28); signifies baptism, CHII 14.321-22, V 1.259-65 (Vf 1.328-35); signifies Christ's body and blood, CHII 15.187-91; signifies the people, CHII 15.249-54; signifies teaching, CHII 25.121-29, Supp 19.30-33; signifies the Jews, Supp 2.115-24; signifies Christ's passion, Supp 2.130-33; signifies turning from idolatry, Supp 5.118-22; water vessel signifies worldly desires, Supp 5.214-24; Moses draws from a stone, Supp 20.22-26; worship of, Supp 21.88, W 12.23; turns bloody on the day of judgement, V 15.55-56 (Vs 15.45-46).

WEALTH: *see also* ALMSGIVING, CLOTHING, COINS, GEMS, GOLD, POVERTY, SILVER, TAXATION, THE

anniversary of Christ's baptism, CHI 7.104.

WERGILD: *see* LAW, MURDER.

WEST: *see also* EAST, NORTH; signifies old age, CHI 8.130; Christ crucified facing, CHII 14.241-42.

WIDOWHOOD: *see also* CELIBACY, MARRIAGE, SEXUALITY, WOMEN; general expositions, CHI 9.148, CHI 30.446-48, CHII 4.294-305, CHII 6.127-31; the widow's mite, CHI 38.582, W 18.91-104; widows compelled to remarry, W 20BH.37-38, W 20C.44-45, W 20EI.42-43.

WILL: *see* FREE WILL.

WINE: *see also* VINEYARD; signifies the New Testament, CHII 4.306-16; vinegar signifies death, CHII 14.222-27; signifies the Jews, CHII 14.284-86; vinegar signifies the Jews, CHII 14.284-86; transubstantiation at the eucharist, CHII 15.86-173.

WINTER: signifies the failure of love during the last days, Supp 18.326-37.

WISDOM: *see also* CHRIST, INTELLECT, PHILOSOPHY, REASON; God created through, CHI 1.10; of Adam, CHI 1.14; made manifest in words, CHI 2.40, CHI 25.362;

signified by gold, CHI 7.116; and innocence, CHI 22.320-22; a gift of the Holy Spirit, CHI 22.322, CHII 25.64-71, Supp 9.139-49, W 9.32-33; the soul the seat of, CHI 35.520; equated with the love and fear of God, CHI 36.550, LS 1.229-39, V 12.51-71 (Vs 12.41-59); granted by God to the unlearned, CHI 38.576-78; of Solomon, CHII 40.20-52; a virtue of the soul, LS 1.155-67, 225-39; the world's wisdom is folly, LS 1.226-28, Supp 16.207-22; the wise should perform good works, LS 13.116; human and divine, LS 13.320-28; gives life to the earth, Supp 1.275-79; and good counsel for kings, Supp 9.36-54; and reason, V 20.159-63 (Vs 20.G18-G21); signified by salt, W 8b.22-25, W 8c.53-56.

THE WISE MEN: *see* THE MAGI.

WOLF: *see also* ANIMALS, FOX; signifies the devil, CHI 17.238-40, Supp 206.209; signifies tyrants, CHI 17.242; St Paul likened to, CHI 27.390; signifies the unconverted, LS 2.98-100; robbers and thieves likened to, LS 19.155-60; guarded St Edmund's head, LS 32.145-47, 154-63; werewolf signifies the devil, W 16b.35.

WOMAN: *see also* THE FALL OF ADAM AND EVE, FORNICATION, MAN,

MARRIAGE, SEXUALITY, WIDOWHOOD; and obedience, CHI 6.98; a woman of faith will be considered a man at God's table, CHI 12.188; peril of wicked women, CHI 32.486, 488; instruments of deceit, CHII 30.125-29; female saints disguise themselves as monks, LS 2.41-53, 88-97, LS 33.93-155; should be modest, LS 13.120; and infanticide, LS 17.148-56; and love potions, LS 17.157-61; luxury and vanity of, V 7.72-82 (Vf 7.79-89).

WORKS: *see* FAITH, GOOD WORKS, LABOUR.

THE WORLD: *see also* THE DAY OF JUDGEMENT, THE EARTH, HEAVEN, HELL, LAST DAYS, LIFE, MAN, WEALTH, WOMEN; all the world awaited Mary's consent at the Annunciation, B 1.7-9; signified by the moon, B 2.17, CHI 10.154, CHII 12.425-38; the darkness of, B 2.17, CHI 18.248, LS 28.108-12; its griefs and uncertainties, B 5.57, CHII 24.215-29, LS 12.82-87, Supp 11.157-59, V 1.117-20 (Vf 1.172-74), V 4.17-31 (Vf 4.19-35); impermanence and failure of, B 5.59, B 10.115, CHI 40.614, LS 5.69-73, LS 12.119-21, LS 16.228-31, 242-45, LS 28.153-56, Supp 10.127-38, V 14.54-62 (Vs 14.44-50), V 22.67-80 (Vs 22.55-65), W 1b.23-24, W 3.14-18, W 4.77-79, W 5.23-32,

W 20BH.1-6, W 20C.7-9, W 20EI.7-11; signified by Lazarus, B 6.75; its evils, B 10.115; the ages of, B 11.117-19, CHI 6.98, CHI 22.312, CHII 4.84-91, CHII 5.60-65, CHII 12.7-16, CHII 15.50-53; CHII 26.80-187, Supp 5.110-12, Supp 21.498-505; its pleasures become griefs after death, B 16.195, CHI 28.408, CHI 35.530; the beginning of, CHI 6.100; the devil the prince of worldly men, CHI 11.172; signified by the sea, CHI 12.182-84, CHII 16.142-52, CHII 24.86-92, 215-29, Supp 14.57-62; the clergy's compromise with, CHI 17.240-42; ignorance of, CHI 18.248; signified by night, CHI 18.248, CHII 39.102-12; love of signified by millstone, CHI 34.514; its falseness, CHI 34.514-16, LS 5.61-68; the distraction of worldly cares, CHI 35.524; contempt for, CHI 40.612-14, LS 28.157-64, V 7.82-83 (Vf 7.89-91), V 14.163-70 (Vs 14.127-33), V 20.180-88 (Vs 20.G34-G40); signified by Babylon, CHII 4.247-67; its history paralleled by the course of human ageing, CHII 5.88-106; worldly cares and the body, CHII 6.90-105; signified by Egypt, CHII 12.178-91; equated with men who love it more than heaven, CHII 22.146-62; worldly desires signified by grass, CHII 25.72-78; its wisdom folly, LS 1.226-28, Supp 16.207-22;

persistence of men's love for,
LS 28.165-70; rejected Christ,
Supp 1.336-49; worldly desires
signified by water vessel,
Supp 5.214-24; devil the prince of,
Supp 7.171-80; values the sinful and
oppresses the righteous, V 22.25-36
(Vs 22.21-29).

WRATH: *see also* HATE, SIN;
general expositions,
CHII 12.510-13, 553-54,
V 20.98-103 (Vs 20.77-81); anger
meant to be directed against sin,
LS 1.102-107; kills the soul if it
rules, LS 1.146-48; signified by
mote in eye, Supp 13.146-61; and
murder, Supp 15.125-42; and insult,
Supp 15.143-56; consequences of,
V 20.99-101 (Vs 20.78-79);
remedied by patience, V 20.101-103
(Vs 20.80-81); God does not hear
the prayers of the wrathful,
W 18.114-23.

Y

YOUTH: *see also* THE BODY,
CHILDREN, OLD AGE; signified by the
east, CHI 8.130; the young should be
obedient, LS 13.118.

APPENDICES

APPENDIX 1
INDEX OF MAJOR NAMES

AARON: *see also* MOSES [index: THE EXODUS, THE JEWS, THE LAW OF MOSES]; and the worship of the golden calf, Supp 20.216-73; his death, Supp 20.365-75; the office of bishop descended from, W 17.19-28.

ST ABDON: *passio*, **Supp 24**.

ABEL: his murder signifies the crucifixion of Christ, CHII 4.104-10; his righteousness, LS 16.13-15, V 7.6-10 (Vf 7.6-12); his murder narrated, W 6.53-56.

ABIGAIL: counsels David against committing murder, CHI 32.482.

ABIRAM: and the worship of the golden calf, LS 13.221-29, Supp 20.216-60.

ABRAHAM: *see also* [index: THE JEWS, THE PATRIARCHS]; calls out to Christ at the Harrowing, B 7.89; Christ made covenant with, B 13.159; and circumcision, CHI 6.90; was wealthy but faithful, CHI 8.130-32; God's promise to, CHI 13.204, CHII 12.17-27; and the beggar Lazarus, CHI 23.330-32; was poor in spirit, CHI 36.550; his sacrifice of Isaac, CHII 4.131-78;

his 'dwelling' in hell, CHII 5.152-55; the Jews virtuous through, CHII 13.66-69; Isaac's oath to, CHII 13.190-204; intercedes for Sodom and Gomorrah, LS 13.192-220, Supp 18.65-74; his faith, LS 16.25-27, V 7.11-17 (Vf 7.12-18); untouched by idolatry, W 6.96-100.

ABSOLOM: his treason, LS 19.196-203.

ACHITOPHEL: gives Absolom treasonous counsel, LS 19.155, 196-214.

ADAM: *see also* EVE [index: THE FALL OF ADAM AND EVE]; released from hell at the harrowing, B 7.87-89, W 15.23-26; creation of, CHI 1.12, 16, CHI 16.236, Supp 21.28-44, V 19.23-29 (Vs 19.19-23), W 6.34-39, W 15.8-18; his wisdom, CHI 1.14; prohibition on the fruit for his own good, CHI 1.14, V 19.31-37 (Vs 19.27-31), W 6.44-52; fall of, CHI 1.16-20, CHI 18.254, CHI 21.300, CHII 1.14-17, 110-18, CHII 31.78-84, Supp 11.94-106, Supp 11a.47-52, V 2.93-95 (Vf 2.122-25), V 14.17-33

(Vs 14.15-27), V 19.37-48
(Vs 19.27-39), V 21.126-29
(Vs 21.97-101), W 6.44-52,
W 10c.78-79; his innocence,
CHI 1.18; his free will, CHI 1.18,
CHI 20.288; his deception by Satan,
CHI 1.18-20, CHI 30.460,
CHII 30.125-29, W 7.37-38; God's
mercy towards, CHI 1.18-20,
W 7.38-49; his resemblance to God,
CHI 20.288; Eve created from his
side, CHII 4.100-104,
CHII 14.323-27, V 19.29-31
(Vs 19.24-26); marks an age of the
world, CHII 4.84-91; his curse,
CHII 31.38-40, LS 12.21-28,
Supp 21.45-55, W 8b.19-21,
W 8c.32-34, W 14.36-40,
W 15.18-23; his presumption,
LS 13.184.

ÆLFLÆD: St Cuthbert warns of
her brother Ecgfrith's impending
death, CHII 10.210-25; St Cuthbert
sees her steward's soul conducted to
heaven, CHII 10.292-303.

ÆTHELBERT: St Augustine's
mission converts, CHII 9.188-225.

ÆTHELRÆD: his exile,
W 20BH.71-72.

ST ÆTHELTHRYTH: *vita*,
Supp 20.

ST ÆTHELWOLD: his reforms,
LS 21.454-63.

ST AGATHA: *passio*, **Supp 8**;
St Lucy's mother cured of
haemorrhage at her tomb, LS 9.1-22;
appears to St Lucy, LS 9.23-35.

ST AGNES: *passio* **Supp 7**.

AHAB: his reign and persecution of
Elijah, LS 18.45-222.

ST AIDAN: St Cuthbert sees his
soul conducted to heaven,
CHII 10.48-51; sent to assist
St Oswald's reforms, LS 26.45-82;
blesses St Oswald's arm,
LS 26.98-103.

ST ALBAN: *passio*, **Supp 19**.

ST ALEXANDER: performs
miracles and effects conversions
under persecution by Trajan,
Supp 23.

ST AMBROSE: excommunicates
then forgives Theodosius I, **Supp 26**.

AMMON: idolatrous king of Israel,
LS 18.452-57.

AMOS: turned by the Holy Spirit
from a cowherd into a prophet,
CHI 22.322.

ANANIAS: seeks to conceal
property from St Peter,
CHI 22.316-18; signifies those who
vacillate about entering into
monastic life, CHI 27.398.

BEELZEBUB: *see* [index: THE DEVIL, DEVILS, EXORCISM].

BEL: *see* [index: IDOLATRY].

ST BENEDICT: *vita*, **CHII 11**; and St Maurus, **Supp 6**.

CAIAPHAS: prophesies unwittingly about Christ, V 1.7-18 (Vf 1.49-61); interrogates Christ, V 1.57-82 (Vf 1.104-32).

CAIN: his murder of Abel signifies the crucifixion of Christ, CHII 4.104-10; his murder of Abel narrated, W 6.53-56.

ST CECILIA: her marriage and martyrdom, **Supp 34**.

ST CHRYSANTHUS: his refutation of pagan philosophy and martyrdom, **Supp 35**.

ST CLEMENT: *vita*, **CHI 37**.

CONSTANTINE: his vision of the cross and conversion, CHII 18.1-37, Supp 26.7-15; builds a church in thanks to St Agnes, LS 7.260-95; delegates military authority to his general Gallicanus, Supp 22.51-58.

CORNELIUS: converted and baptized by St Peter, LS 10.109-71.

ST CUTHBERT: *vita*, **CHII 10**.

CYRINUS: his name means 'heir', CHI 2.32-34; signifies St Peter, V 5.106-15 (Vf 5.122-32).

CYRUS: puts Daniel into the lions' den, CHI 37.570-72, Supp 21.350-431; ends the Babylonian captivity, W 6.122-27.

DANIEL: in the lions' den, CHI 32.488, CHI 37.570-72, LS 16.78-82, Supp 21.300-49, 451-93, V 3.136-37 (Vf 3.150-51); Bel and the dragon, Supp 21.350-450.

ST DARIA: his renunciation of pagan philosophy and martyrdom, **Supp 35**.

DARIUS: throws Daniel to the lions, Supp 21.300-49.

DATHAN: and the worship of the golden calf, LS 13.221-29, Supp 20.216-60.

DAVID: his slaying of Goliath signifies Christ's defeat of the devil, B 3.31; Christ as the son of, CHI 14.214; inspired to write the psalms by the Holy Spirit, CHI 22.322; was poor in spirit, CHI 36.550; chosen by Samuel to succeed Saul, CHII 4.179-209; executes man who falsely confessed to killing Saul, LS 12.247-53; God punished his sins with a plague, LS 13.240-72; his humility,

LS 16.55-59; summary of his career, LS 18.13-36; Absalom's treason to, LS 19.196-203; delegates military authority to Joab, Supp 22.13-50; his fasting, V 3.107-10 (Vf 3.118-21); his glory, W 6.106-10; and the building of Solomon's temple, W 18.6-19.

DECIUS: tortures St Lawrence for location of church treasure, **CHI 29**.

DELILAH: example of evil woman CHI 32.488.

ST DIONYSUS (ST DENIS): his life and martyrdom, CHI 37.558-60; **Supp 29**.

DIVES: and Lazarus, CHI 23.328-34.

DOMITIAN: his persecution of St John the Evangelist, CHI 4.58-60, CHI 37.574.

DRIHTHELM: his vision of the afterlife, **CHII 21**.

ST DUNSTAN: and Æthelwold's reforms, LS 21.454-63.

ECGFRITH: his death predicted by St Cuthbert, CHII 10.210-25; persuades St Cuthbert to become a bishop, CHII 10.239-52.

ST EDMUND: *passio*, **Supp 32**.

EDWARD: his murder, W 20BH.70-71, W20C.82-83, W 20EI.77-78.

ELIJAH: his fasting, CHI 11.178, CHII 7.13-16, Supp 2.154-57; his charity, CHI 21.308; will return to combat Antichrist, CHI 21.306-308, CHI 25.356, CHII 7.16-18, W 5.88-96; fed by a raven, CHII 10.103-106; summary of his career, LS 16.60-70, LS 18.45-299; prays for drought, Supp 8.79-84, V 3.133-35 (Vf 3.145-148), V 20.16-22 (Vs 20.13-18).

ELISHA: refuses to heal for money, CHI 27.400; succeeds to office of Elijah, LS 18.276-356.

ELIZABETH: and the birth of John the Baptist, B 14.161-63, CHI 13.200-202, CHI 25.352-54.

ENOCH: will return to combat Antichrist, CHI 21.306-308, LS 16.16-21, W 5.88-96; his chastity, CHI 21.308.

ESAU: his different fate from Jacob's disproves astrology, CHI 7.110; his character, V 7.43-45 (Vf 7.47-50).

ST EUGENIA: *vita* **Supp 2**.

ST EUPHRASIA: *vita* **Supp 33**.

ST EUSTACE: *vita* **Supp 30**.

in scripture, CHII 24.42-52.

HEROD: and the death of St John the Baptist, CHI 32.478-88; interviews Christ, CHII 14.169-76; one of three scriptural Herods, CHII 24.42-52.

HERODIAS: and the death of St John the Baptist, CHI 32.478, 482-88.

HEZEKIAH: Isaiah cures, CHI 31.474-76; prays for Israel's deliverance from Sennacherib, CHI 37.568-70, LS 18.386-433; prays to be healed of illness, V 3.137-39 (Vf 3.151-52).

ST HILARY: instructs St Martin, B 18.217, CHII 34.59-64, 91-94, LS 31.201-206, V 18.82-93 (Vs 18.66-74).

HORSA: invades Britain, LS 19.147-54.

ISAAC: *see also* ABRAHAM, SARAH [index: THE JEWS, THE PATRIARCHS]; Abraham offers as a sacrifice, CHII 4.131-78; his oath sworn on Abraham's thigh, CHII 13.190-204.

ISAIAH: cures Hezekiah, CHI 31.474-76; prophesies Israel's deliverance from Sennacherib, CHI 37.568-70; summary of his ministry, W 11.99-117; his denunciation of thieves and the covetous, W 11.118-24, 133-39; his denunciation of pride, W 11.125-32; his denunciation of gluttony and drunkenness, W 11.140-49; his denunciation of false counsellors, W 11.150-55.

ISRAEL: *see also* JACOB [index: THE JEWS]; means 'seeing God', CHI 13.198.

JACOB: *see also* [index: THE JEWS, THE PATRIARCHS]; his different fate from Esau's disproves astrology, CHI 7.110; 'Jacob' means 'withering', CHI 13.198; was poor in spirit, CHI 36.550; his migration to Egypt, CHII 12.28-40; his faith, LS 16.29-35.

ST JAMES: occupied Christ's seat for thirty years, CHI 22.318, CHII 17.70-71; his community leaves Jerusalem after his martyrdom, CHI 28.402; 'James' means 'withering', CHI 38.586; *vita*, **CHII 17**; cousin of Christ, Supp 14.207-13.

ST JAMES (BROTHER OF ST JOHN THE EVANGELIST): *vita*, **CHII 27**; martyrdom, CHII 24.1-6, CHI 35.524, CHII 37.137-54.

JEHORAM: his reign, LS 18.268-72, 315-36.

JEHU: slays Jezebel and the priests of Baal, LS 18.313-85.

also [index: THE JEWS, THE PATRIARCHS]; and Jacob's migration to Egypt, CHII 12.28-40.

JOSHUA: bowed and prayed to angels, CHI 2.38; and the conquest of the promised land, CHII 12.375-413, 477-92, LS 13.1-29, Supp 20.170-202; signifies Christ, CHII 12.414-24; sun stands still for, CHII 12.565-71; and Moses, Supp 22.87-90.

JOSIAH: his reign, LS 18.458-72.

JUDAS: his betrayal of Christ, B 5.63, CHII 14.14-22, 54-63, 78-83, V 1E.74-112 (Vf 1.1-35); his hypocrisy, B 6.69; once performed miracles, CHI 21.306; the companion of those who defraud monasteries, CHI 27.398; will not be forgiven on the day of judgement, LS 27.157-83.

JUDAS MACCABEUS: *see* THE MACCABEES.

ST JUDE: evangelizing and martyrdom, **CHII 33**.

ST JULIAN: *passio* **Supp 4**.

JULIAN THE APOSTATE: his antagonism toward St Basil, CHI 30.448-50, **Supp 3**; his death, CHI 30.450-52, LS 3.241-76, LS 7.419-20; his persecutions, LS 7.394-420; conscripted priests

and monks into the army, LS 25.833-35, LS 31.98-117; dispatches a devil on an errand, Supp 8.132-52.

JUNO: *see* [index: IDOLATRY].

JUPITER: see [index: IDOLATRY].

ST LAWRENCE: *passio*, **CHI 29**; undue curiosity about the state of his remains, LS 32.239-46.

LAZARUS: Christ raises from the dead, B 6.67, CHI 33.494-96, Supp 6.1-128; signifies the world, B 6.75; loosening of his graveclothes signifies forgiveness of sin, CHI 16.234; signifies one death of the soul, CHI 33.496-98; signifies sinful man, Supp 6.196-208.

LAZARUS: and Dives, CHI 23.328-34.

LOT: bowed and prayed to angels, CHI 2.38; and the destruction of Sodom, Supp 18.65-74.

ST LUCY: *passio*, **Supp 9**.

ST LUKE: and the writing of his gospel, LS 15.150-58; signified by a calf, LS 15.192-96; a spiritual as well as a bodily physician, Supp 13.1-7.

THE MACCABEES: their revolt, **Supp 25**.

and the writing of his gospel,
CHI 22.324, LS 15.127-140;
'Matthew' means 'given',
CHII 32.19-21; wrote about Christ's
human nature, LS 15.184-86; *vita*,
CHII 32.

ST MAURICE: *passio*, **Supp 28.**

ST MAURUS: participates in
St Benedict's miraculous healing of
a child, CHII 11.92-108; *vita*,
Supp 6.

MAXENTIUS: his war with
Constantine, CHII 18.7-37.

MAXIMUS: St Martin accepts his
hospitality and predicts his death,
LS 31.610-49.

MERCURY: *see* [index: IDOLATRY].

ST MICHAEL: *see also* GABRIEL,
RAPHAEL [index: ANGELS]; fights
devils on the day of judgement,
B 7.93-95; orders horns blown for
the day of judgement, B 7.95; the
chief of the angels, B 13.147; at
Mary's assumption, B 13.147,
155-57; appeals to Christ for a
portion of the damned on the day of
judgement, V 15.150-59
(Vs 15.118-25).

MINERVA: *see* [index: IDOLATRY].

MISHAEL: in the fiery furnace,
CHI 37.570, CHII 1.230-66.

MOSES: *see also* AARON [index: THE
EXODUS, THE JEWS, THE LAW OF
MOSES]; was taught by Christ,
B 4.45; punishes the impious,
B 4.49; his fasting, CHI 11.178,
CHII 7.10-13, Supp 2.151-53,
V 3.106-107 (Vf 3.117-18);
transcribed Pentateuch at God's
dictation, CHI 12.186; and the
Exodus, CHII 12.41-119,
LS 13.1-29, Supp 1.364-75,
Supp 22.87-90, W 19.41-59;
receives the Decalogue,
CHII 12.120-48, W 10c.20-31; his
prayer for Israelite victory, **Supp 13**;
and the bronze serpent,
Supp 12.224-38, Supp 20.329-52;
and the golden calf, Supp 20.41-67,
261-73; his death, Supp 20.365-75;
his prayer, V 3.131-33
(Vf 3.143-45); made Aaron the first
bishop, W 17.19-28.

NEBUCHADNEZZAR: and the
Hebrew youths in the fiery furnace,
CHI 37.570, CHII 1.222-66; and the
Babylonian captivity,
CHII 4.210-23; his pride humbled,
CHII 28.96-133.

NERO: and the contest between
St Peter and St Paul and Simon
Magus, **B 15**, CHI 26.370-84; his
death, CHI 35.524.

NERVA: recalls St John the
Evangelist from Patmos, CHI 4.60.

NICODEMUS: buries Christ,

SERAPIS: *see* [index: IDOLATRY].

SIMON PETER: *see* ST PETER.

ST SIMON: evangelizing and martyrdom, **CHII 33**.

SIMON MAGUS: exposed by St Peter and St Paul, **B 15**, CHI 26.370-82; an example of the evil of sorcery, LS 17.118-21.

SOLOMON: his request for wisdom, CHII 40.20-52; builds the temple, CHII 40.52-74, 85-93, W 18.6-19, 91-104; 'Solomon' means 'peaceful', CHII 40.74-85; signifies Christ, CHII 40.74-85, 131-37, 181-87, W 6.66-69; and the Queen of Sheba, CHII 40.147-200.

ST STEPHEN: his martyrdom, **CHI 3**, CHI 21.308-10, CHI 27.384-86, Supp 19.230-35; miracles caused by his relics, **CHII 2**; and St Paul, CHII 5.200-204.

ST SWITHUN: miracles of, **Supp 21**.

THE SYBIL: *see* [index: PROPHECY].

ST THEODOLUS: *passio*, CHII 18.62-156.

THEODOSIUS: delegated military matters to his generals, Supp 22.73-79; St Ambrose

excommunicates, **Supp 26**.

ST THOMAS: his doubt preordained for the benefit of subsequent believers, CHI 16.234-36; a doubtful episode in his *passio*, CHII 34.(additional)7-17; *vita*, **Supp 36**.

THOR: *see* [index: IDOLATRY].

TIBERIUS: Caesarea built in honour of, CHI 26.364-66.

TITUS: destroyed Jerusalem, B 6.79, CHI 28.402-404.

TOBIAS: Raphael conveyed his prayer to God, CHI 34.518.

TOBIT: Raphael explains to him the keeping and revealing of God's secrets, LS 23b.6-18.

TRAJAN: his persecution of Christians, CHI 37.560, 562-64.

VALENS: a heretical emperor, LS 3.292-323.

VALENTINIAN: Arian emperor, confronts St Martin, LS 31.650-81.

VENUS: *see* [index: IDOLATRY].

VESPASIAN: dispatches Titus to Jerusalem, CHI 28.402.

ST VINCENT: *passio*, **Supp 37**.

XERXES: honours the bodies of
St Simon and St Jude,
CHII 33.260-74.

ZACCHEUS: his charity,
CHI 8.130-32, CHI 38.580-82;
climbs a tree to see Christ,
CHI 38.580, Supp 16.173-82.

ZACHARIAS: and the birth of
St John the Baptist, B 14.161-63,
CHI 13.200-202; 'Zacharias' means
'mindful of God', CHI 25.354.

APPENDIX 2

INDEX OF MAJOR PLACE NAMES

MT AETNA: its eruption stilled by a veil from the tomb of St Agatha, LS 8.217-34.

ALEXANDRIA: repository of bones of St John the Baptist, CHI 32.486; growth of Christianity in, LS 2.270-79; destruction of its temple to Serapis, Supp 21.521-27.

ATHENS: St Basil studies philosophy in, LS 3.1-15; St Paul converts St Dionysus in, LS 29.1-5.

BABEL: see BABYLON [index: THE TOWER OF BABEL].

BABYLON: Israel's captivity in, CHI 37.568-72, CHII 4.210-67, CHII 5.233-52, W 6.115-22, W 11.105-17.

BETHLEHEM: see also ST JOSEPH, MARY, THE MOTHER OF CHRIST [index: THE NATIVITY]; means 'house of bread', CHI 2.34, V 5.116-24 (Vf 5.133-41).

BETHPAGE: signifies the Church, B 6.77.

CAESAREA: Philip the Tetrarch built in honour of Tiberius, CHI 26.364-66.

CANA: the wedding at, CHI 4.58, **CHII 4**; means 'enmity', CHII 4.37-44.

CRETE: site of the 'real' Saturn's outrages, Supp 21.104-12, W 12.39-44.

DAMASCUS: see [index: ST PAUL].

EGYPT: see also [index: THE EXODUS, THE NATIVITY]; ascetic saints in, CHI 36.546; the patriarchs in, CHII 12.28-101; signifies the world, CHII 12.178-91; pharaoh signifies the devil, CHII 12.178-91; its idols fall at the approach of the infant Christ, V 6.69-80 (Vf 6.78-90); its kings now in torment, V 7.46-49 (Vf 7.50-53).

ENGLAND: its location on the world's periphery, LS 13.106-109; its contemporary woes, LS 13.147-55, **W 20BH, W 20C, W 20EI**; likened to Israel, LS 13.175-81.

EPHESUS: see [index: THE SEVEN

death in, CHI 30.448-50; guiding
angel of, CHI 34.518.
THE RED SEA: *see* [index: THE
EXODUS, THE JEWS, PASSOVER].

ROME: St Peter and St Paul
contend with Simon Magus there,
B 15, CHI 26.370-84.

SAMARIA: 'Samaritan' means
'shepherd', CHII 13.102-104;
signifies the gentiles, Supp 5.113-17;
general description, CHII 13.96-104.

SIDON: its repentance,
Supp 17.51-66.

SINAI: *see* [appendix 1: MOSES; index:
THE JEWS, THE LAW OF MOSES].

SODOM: *see also* GOMORRAH
[appendix 1: ABRAHAM, LOT; index:
SEXUALITY, FORNICATION]; Jews
blinded at Mary's funeral fear the
fate of, B 13.153; Abraham's
intercession for, LS 13.192-206,
Supp 18.65-74; corruption of,
V 7.38-43 (Vf 7.42-47).

THESSALONIKA: St Ambrose
excommunicates Theodosius I for the
destruction of, **Supp 26**.

TOURS: St Martin made bishop of,
LS 31.254-66, V 18.139-53
(Vs 18.C20-91); strife with Poitiers
over possession of St Martin's body,
LS 31.1441-92.

TYRE: its repentance,
Supp 17.51-66.

THE VATICAN: angels bury
St Peter there, B 15.191-93.

VIENNA: Mamertus turns the
plague from with fasting,
CHI 18.244, V 19.149-64
(Vs 19.117-29).

ZION: means 'place of
contemplation', CHI 14.210.

APPENDIX 3

CHECKLIST OF PRIMARY TOPICS AND OCCASIONS

B 1: The Annunciation

B 2: Spiritual blindness

B 3: The Temptation of Christ

B 4: Tithes, clerical duties

B 5: Body and soul, honesty, envy
and slander

B 6: Palm Sunday

B 7: Easter, the harrowing of hell

B 8: Body and soul

B 9: The Incarnation

B 10: Death and the transience of
the world

B 11: The Ascension

B 12: Pentecost

B 13: The Assumption of Mary

B 14: The birth of St John the
Baptist

B 15: St Peter, St Paul, Simon
Magus

B 16: The vanity of worldly wealth

B 17: The Church of St Michael

B 18: St Martin

B 19: St Andrew

CHI pref: Translation, last days,
Antichrist

CHI 1: Salvation history

CHI 2: The Nativity

CHI 3: The passion of St Stephen

CHI 4: The Assumption of St John

CHI 5: The Holy Innocents

CHI 6: The Circumcision of Christ

CHI 7: The Magi, free will, and the
fall of Adam and Eve

CHI 8: Faith and humility, the
symbolism of Christ's healing of
a leper

CHI 9: The Purification of Mary

CHI 10: Blindness and light, the blind man on the road to Jericho

CHI 11: The temptation of Christ

CHI 12: The miracle of the loaves and fish

CHI 13: The Annunciation

CHI 14: Palm Sunday

CHI 15: Easter

CHI 16: The Resurrection of Christ

CHI 17: The shepherds of the Church

CHI 18: Prayer and charity, origins of Rogationtide practices

CHI 19: The Lord's Prayer

CHI 20: The Christian faith

CHI 21: The Ascension

CHI 22: Pentecost

CHI 23: Dives and Lazarus, care for the poor

CHI 24: Grace, the fall of the angels and their ranks

CHI 25: St John the Baptist

CHI 26: St Peter's faith and authority, St Paul, Simon Magus

CHI 27: The conversion of St Paul, numerological symbolism

CHI 28: The Roman sack of Jerusalem

CHI 29: The passion of St Lawrence

CHI 30: The Assumption of Mary

CHI 31: St Bartholomew, disease and healing

CHI 32: The death of St John the Baptist

CHI 33: The widow of Nain's son, the deaths of the soul, repentance

CHI 34: The Church of St Michael

CHI 35: The Church and the Kingdom of Heaven

CHI 36: Saints, the Beatitudes

CHI 37: St Clement

CHI 38: St Andrew

CHI 39: Advent, sins

CHI 40: The last days

CHII 1: The Nativity, virginity, prophecies of Christ

CHII 2: The miracles of St Stephen

CHII 3: Christ's baptism, humility, the Trinity

CHII 4: The Wedding at Cana, the ages of the world

CHII 5: The parable of the vineyard workers, the ages of the world

CHII 6: The sower and the seed, patience and chastity

CHII 7: Lent, almsgiving

CHII 8: Christians and Jews

CHII 9: St Gregory

CHII 10: St Cuthbert

CHII 11: St Benedict

CHII 12: The Heptateuch, the eight deadly sins

CHII 13: Christ and the Jews

CHII 14: The Passion

CHII 15: Easter, the Eucharist

CHII 16: The Resurrection of Christ, the road to Emmaeus

CHII 17: St Philip and St James

CHII 18: Invention of the cross,

St Eventius and St Theodolus

CHII 19: Love and the structure of society

CHII 20: Fursey's vision of the afterlife

CHII 21: Drihthelm's vision of the afterlife

CHII 22: Christ's eucharistic prayer in St John's gospel, the relationship between the Father and the Son

CHII 23: The parable of the feast and the reluctant invitees, God's summons

CHII 24: St Peter

CHII 25: The miracle of the loaves and fish

CHII 26: Hypocrisy, repentance, wealth

CHII 27: St James (the brother of St John the Evangelist)

CHII 28: Pride and humility

CHII 29: Active and contemplative life, the Assumption of Mary

CHII 30: Job

CHII 31: God and Mammon, body

and soul

CHII 32: St Matthew

CHII 33: St Simon, St Jude

CHII 34: St Martin

CHII 35: The apostles, the faithful, prayer

CHII 36: Teachers

CHII 37: Patience, persecution, martyrdom

CHII 38: The parable of the talents

CHII 39: The parable of the wise and foolish virgins, virginity, the day of judgement

CHII 40: The Temple of Solomon and the Church

LS 1: The Nativity, the soul, the Trinity

LS 2: St Eugenia

LS 3: St Basil

LS 4: St Julian and St Basilissa

LS 5: St Sebastian

LS 6: St Maurus

LS 7: St Agnes

LS 8: St Agatha

LS 9: St Lucy

LS 10: St Peter, the conversion of gentiles, virginity

LS 11: The Forty Soldiers

LS 12: Fasting, repentance, Lenten observances, confession, prayer

LS 13: The Exodus, prayer, fasting, right behaviour

LS 14: St George

LS 15: St Mark

LS 16: The Trinity, salvation history, martyrs, heresy, the eight deadly sins

LS 17: Augury, sorcery, reason, free will

LS 18: The kings of Israel

LS 19: St Alban, Absolom and Achitophel

LS 20: St Æthelthryth

LS 21: St Swithun, sorcery

LS 22: St Apollinaris

LS 23: The Seven Sleepers of Ephesus

LS 23b: St Mary of Egypt

LS 24: St Abdon, St Sennes,
Christ's letter to Abgarus

LS 25: The Maccabees

LS 26: St Oswald

LS 27: The invention of the cross
and its later adventures

LS 28: St Maurice and his
companions

LS 29: St Dionysus and his
companions

LS 30: St Eustace and his
companions

LS 31: St Martin

LS 32: St Edmund

LS 33: St Euphrasia

LS 34: St Cecilia

LS 35: St Chrysanthus and St Daria

LS 36: St Thomas

LS 37: St Vincent

Supp 1: The Nativity, the gospel of
St John, the Trinity, the Fall,
Christ the Logos

Supp 2: The paralytic at the pool,
the spiritual meaning of
handicaps

Supp 3: Christ the cornerstone, the
vineyard workers and the
owner's messengers

Supp 4: Exorcism, the devil

Supp 5: Jews and Christians, sowers
and reapers

Supp 6: The raising of Lazarus, the
Trinity

Supp 7: The risen Christ, the Holy
Spirit

Supp 8: Prayer, Christ

Supp 9: Kings, the Trinity

Supp 10: Pentecost

Supp 11: Church holy days

Supp 12: Baptism, Nicodemus

Supp 13: Forgiveness, teaching,
hypocrisy

Supp 14: St Peter the fisherman

Supp 15: Forgiveness, the Old and
New Testaments

Supp 16: Reason, almsgiving

Supp 17: Conversion and repentance, devils

Supp 18: The last days

Supp 19: Teaching, chastity, despair

Supp 20: The nation of Israel

Supp 21: False gods

Supp 22: Kings and generals

Supp 23: St Alexander, St Eventius, St Theodolus,

Supp 24: Oaths

Supp 25: Christians

Supp 26: Theodosius I and St Ambrose

Supp 27: Repentance, death

Supp 28: Antichrist

Supp 29: Saul and the witch of Endor

Supp 30: Humility, tithing

V 1 (Vf 1): The Passion

V 2 (Vf 2): The day of judgement

V 3 (Vf 3): Repentance, fasting, prayer, almsgiving

V 4 (Vf 4): Hell and sinners, the last judgement

V 5 (Vf 5): The Nativity

V 6 (Vf 6): The Nativity

V 7 (Vf 7): Abstinence, luxury and gluttony

V 8 (Vf 8): Confession and the last judgement

V 9 (Vs 9): Death, heaven and hell

V 10 (Vs 10): Judgement, almsgiving

V 11 (Vs 11): Rogationtide observances, the Fall, redemption

V 12 (Vs 12): Rogationtide observances, the fear of God, repentance

V 13 (Vs 13): Death

V 14 (Vs 14): Repentance and forgiveness, sins and virtues

V 15 (Vs 15): The day of judgement

V 16 (Vs 16): The baptism of Christ, the Trinity

V 17 (Vs 17): The Purification of Mary

V 18 (Vs 18): St Martin

V 19 (Vs 19): The creation and fall of man, sin, penance during Rogationtide

V 20 (Vs 20): Fasting, tithing, almsgiving, the eight deadly sins and their corresponding virtues

V 21 (Vs 21): Sins and virtues, the day of judgement

V 22 (Vs 22): Repentance, death

V 23 (Vs 23): St Guthlac

W 1b: Antichrist

W 2: The last days

W 3: The last days and the day of judgement

W 4: Antichrist

W 5: The last days

W 6: salvation history

W 7: The Christian faith

W 7a: The *pater noster* and the *credo*

W 8b: Christening, baptism, the Eucharist

W 8c: Christening, baptism, the Eucharist, faith

W 9: gifts of the spirit, hypocrisy

W 10a: monastic conduct

W 10c: Christianity, sins and virtues

W 11: Sin and repentance

W 12: False gods

W 13: Christian conduct

W 14: Lenten observances

W 15: Excommunication and penance

W 16b: Clergy, teachers

W 17: Bishops

W 18: The Temple of Solomon and the Church

W 19: The disobedience and repentance of Israel

W 20BH, C, EI: contemporary woes and the last days

W 21: Divine and secular law

About the Author

Robert DiNapoli received his M.A. in English literature and linguistics from the University of Delaware and Ph.D. in English from the University of Toronto. At present he is a part-time lecturer and tutor in Old and Middle English at Lancaster University and the University of Manchester.

The Hallowing of England
A Guide to the Saints of Old England and their Places of Pilgrimage
Fr. Andrew Philips

In the Old English period we can count over 300 saints, yet today their names and exploits are largely unknown. They are part of a forgotten England which, though it lies deep in the past, is an important part of our national and spiritual history. This guide includes a list of saints, an alphabetical list of places with which they are associated, and a calendar of saint's feast days.

UK £4·95 net   ISBN 1–898281–08–4   96pp

The Service of Prime from the
Old English Benedictine Office
Text and Translation - Prepared by Bill Griffiths

The Old English Benedictine Office was a series of monastic daily services compiled in the late tenth or early eleventh centuries from the material that had largely already been translated from Latin into Old English. From that collection this version of the Old English Service of Prime was prepared for performance at the Anglo-Saxon church of St. Peter-on-the-Wall at Bradwell-on-Sea, Essex on 10th August 1991.

UK £2·50 net   ISBN0–9516209–3–2   40pp

Looking for the Lost Gods of England
Kathleen Herbert

Kathleen Herbert sifts through the royal genealogies, charms, verse and other sources to find clues to the names and attributes of the Gods and Goddesses of the early English. The earliest account of English heathen practices reveals that they worshipped the Earth Mother and called her Nerthus. The tales, beliefs and traditions of that time are still with us and able to stir our minds and imaginations.

UK £4·95 net   ISBN 1–898281–04–1   64pp

Anglo-Saxon Verse Charms, Maxims
and Heroic Legends
Louis J. Rodrigues

The Germanic tribes who settled in Britain during the fifth and early sixth centuries brought with them a store of heroic and folk traditions: folk-tales, legends, rune-lore, magic charms against misfortune and illness, herbal cures, and the homely wisdom of experience enshrined in maxims and gnomic verse. Louis Rodrigues looks at the heroic and folk traditions that were recorded in verse, and which have managed to survive the depredations of time.

UK £7·95 net   ISBN 1–898281–01–7   176pp

Wordcraft
Concise English/Old English Dictionary and Thesaurus
Stephen Pollington

This book provides Old English equivalents to the commoner modern words in both dictionary and thesaurus formats. The Thesaurus presents vocabulary relevant to a wide range of individual topics in alphabetical lists, thus making it easily accessible to those with specific areas of interest. Each thematic listing is encoded for cross-reference from the Dictionary. The two sections will be of invaluable assistance to students of the language, as well as to those with either a general or a specific interest in the Anglo-Saxon period.

UK £9·95 net ISBN 1–898281–02–5 256pp

Spellcraft
Old English Heroic Legends
Kathleen Herbert

The author has taken the skeletons of ancient Germanic legends about great kings, queens and heroes, and put flesh on them. Kathleen Herbert's extensive knowledge of the period is reflected in the wealth of detail she brings to these tales of adventure, passion, bloodshed and magic.

The book is in two parts. First are the stories that originate deep in the past, yet because they have not been hackneyed, they are still strange and enchanting. After that there is a selection of the source material, with information about where it can be found and some discussion about how it can be used.

UK £6·95 net ISBN 0–9516209–9–1 288pp

Monasteriales Indicia
The Anglo-Saxon Monastic Sign Language
Edited with notes and translation by
Debby Banham

The *Monasteriales Indicia* is one of very few texts which let us see how life was really lived in monasteries in the early Middle Ages. Written in Old English and preserved in a manuscript of the mid-eleventh century, it consists of 127 signs used by Anglo-Saxon monks during the times when the Benedictine Rule forbade them to speak. These indicate the foods the monks ate, the clothes they wore, and the books they used in church and chapter, as well as the tools they used in their daily life, and persons they might meet both in the monastery and outside. The text is printed here with a parallel translation.

UK £6·95 net ISBN 0–9516209–4–0 96pp

A Handbook of Anglo-Saxon Food:
Processing and Consumption
Ann Hagen

For the first time information from various sources has been brought together in order to build up a picture of how food was grown, conserved, prepared and eaten during the period from the beginning of the 5th century to the 11th century. Many people will find it fascinating for the views it gives of an important aspect of Anglo-Saxon life and culture. In addition to Anglo-Saxon England the Celtic west of Britain is also covered. Now with an extensive index.

UK £7·95 net ISBN 0-9516209-8-3 192pp

A Second Handbook of Anglo-Saxon Food & Drink:
Production & Distribution
Ann Hagen

Food production for home consumption was the basis of economic activity throughout the Anglo-Saxon period. This second handbook complements the first and brings together a vast amount of information on livestock, cereal and vegetable crops, fish, honey and fermented drinks. Related subjects such as hospitality, charity and drunkenness are also dealt with. With an extensive index.

UK £14·95 net ISBN 1-898281-12-2 432pp

Anglo-Saxon Runes
John. M. Kemble

Kemble's essay *On Anglo-Saxon Runes* first appeared in the journal *Archaeologia* for 1840; it draws on the work of Wilhelm Grimm, but breaks new ground for Anglo-Saxon studies in his survey of the Ruthwell Cross and the Cynewulf poems. For this edition, new notes have been supplied, which include translations of Latin and Old English material quoted in the text, to make this key work in the study of runes more accessible to the general reader.

UK £6·95 net ISBN 0-9516209-1-6 80pp

The Battle of Maldon: Text and Translation
Translated and edited by Bill Griffiths

The Battle of Maldon was fought between the men of Essex and the Vikings in AD 991. The action was captured in an Anglo-Saxon poem whose vividness and heroic spirit has fascinated readers and scholars for generations. *The Battle of Maldon* includes the source text; edited text; parallel literal translation; verse translation; review of 103 books and articles.

UK £4·95 net ISBN 0-9516209-0-8 96pp

Anglo-Saxon Riddles

Translated by John Porter

This is a book full of ingenious characters who speak their names in riddles. Here you will meet a one-eyed garlic seller, a bookworm, an iceberg, an oyster, the sun and moon and a host of others from the everyday life and imagination of the Anglo-Saxons.

Their sense of the awesome power of creation goes hand in hand with a frank delight in obscenity, a fascination with disguise and with the mysterious processes by which the natural world is turned to human use.

John Porter's sparkling translations retain all the vigour and subtly of the original Old English poems, transporting us back over a thousand years to the roots of our language and literature.

This edition contains all 95 riddles of the Exeter Book.

£4·95   ISBN 1–898281–13–0   112pp

Rudiments of Runelore

Stephen Pollington

The purpose of this book is to provide both a comprehensive introduction for those coming to the subject for the first time, and a handy and inexpensive reference work for those with some knowledge of the subject. The *Abecedarium Nordmannicum* and the English, Norwegian and Icelandic rune poems are included in their original and translated form. Also included are the Cynewulf poems, two rune riddles, and new work on the three Brandon runic inscriptions and the Norfolk 'Tiw' runes.

UK £5·95 net   ISBN 1–898281–16–5   Illustrations   104pp

Early English Laws 650–875

Bill Griffiths

Much of Anglo-Saxon life followed a traditional pattern, of custom, and of dependence on kin-groups for land, support and security. The Viking incursions of the ninth century and the reconquest of the north that followed both disturbed this pattern and led to a new emphasis on centralized power and law, with royal and ecclesiastical officials prominent as arbitrators and settlers of disputes.

The diversity and development of early English law is sampled here by selecting several law-codes to be read in translation - that of Æthelbert of Kent, being the first to be issued in England, Alfred the Great's, the most clearly thought-out of all, and short codes from the reigns of Edmund and Æthelred the Unready.

£6·95 net   ISBN 1–898281–14–9   96pp

Alfred's Metres of Boethius
Edited by Bill Griffiths

In this new edition of the Old English *Metres of Boethius*, clarity of text, informative notes and a helpful glossary have been a priority, for this is one of the most approachable of Old English verse texts, lucid and delightful; its relative neglect by specialists will mean this text will come as a new experience to many practised students of the language; while its clear, expositional verse style makes it an ideal starting point for all amateurs of the period. The texts are in O. E. with an Introduction and Notes in Modern English.

UK £14·95 net ISBN 1–898281–03–3 B5 212pp

Beowulf: Text and Translation
Translated by John Porter

The verse in which the story unfolds is, by common consent, the finest writing surviving in Old English, a text that all students of the language and many general readers will want to tackle in the original form. To aid understanding of the Old English, a literal word-by-word translation by John Porter is printed opposite an edited text and provides a practical key to this Anglo-Saxon masterpiece.

UK £7·95 net ISBN 0–9516209–2–4 192pp

An Introduction to
The Old English Language and its Literature
Stephen Pollington

The purpose of this general introduction to Old English is not to deal with the teaching of Old English but to dispel some misconceptions about the language and to give an outline of its structure and its literature. Some basic knowledge of these is essential to an understanding of the early period of English history and the present form of the language.

UK £2·95 net ISBN 1–898281–06–8 28pp

We accept payment by cheque, Visa, Eurocard and Mastercard.
For orders totalling less than £5 please add 50 pence for post and packing in the UK.
For a full list of publications and overseas postal charges send a s.a.e. to:

Anglo-Saxon Books
Frithgarth, Thetford Forest Park, Hockwold cum Wilton, Norfolk IP26 4NQ
Tel/Fax: 01842 828430

Most titles are available in North America from:
Paul & Company Publishers Consortium Inc.
c/o PCS Data Processing Inc., 360 West 31 St., New York, NY 10001
Tel: (212) 564-3730 ext. 264